THE COMPLETE DICTIONARY OF

ACCOUNTING

AND

BOOKKEEPING TERMS

Explained Simply

By Cindy Ferraino

THE COMPLETE DICTIONARY OF ACCOUNTING & BOOKKEEPING TERMS EXPLAINED SIMPLY

Copyright © 2011 Atlantic Publishing Group, Inc.
1405 SW 6th Avenue • Ocala, Florida 34471 • Phone 800-814-1132 • Fax 352-622-1875
Web site: www.atlantic-pub.com • E-mail: sales@atlantic-pub.com
SAN Number: 268-1250

Library of Congress Cataloging-in-Publication Data

Ferraino, Cindy.
  The complete dictionary of accounting & bookkeeping terms explained simply / by Cindy Ferraino.
    p. cm.
  Includes bibliographical references.
  ISBN-13: 978-1-60138-325-9 (alk. paper)
  ISBN-10: 1-60138-325-8 (alk. paper)
  1. Accounting--Dictionaries. 2. Bookkeeping--Dictionaries. 3. Terms and phrases. I. Title.
  HF5636.F47 2010
  657.03--dc22
                            2010039119

Printed in the United States

Printed on Recycled Paper

PROJECT MANAGER: Shannon McCarthy
PEER REVIEWER: Marilee Griffin
FRONT & BACK COVER DESIGN: Jackie Miller • millerjackiej@gmail.com

We recently lost our beloved pet "Bear," who was not only our best and dearest friend but also the "Vice President of Sunshine" here at Atlantic Publishing. He did not receive a salary but worked tirelessly 24 hours a day to please his parents. Bear was a rescue dog that turned around and showered myself, my wife, Sherri, his grandparents Jean, Bob, and Nancy, and every person and animal he met (maybe not rabbits) with friendship and love. He made a lot of people smile every day.

We wanted you to know that a portion of the profits of this book will be donated to The Humane Society of the United States. *–Douglas & Sherri Brown*

The human-animal bond is as old as human history. We cherish our animal companions for their unconditional affection and acceptance. We feel a thrill when we glimpse wild creatures in their natural habitat or in our own backyard.

Unfortunately, the human-animal bond has at times been weakened. Humans have exploited some animal species to the point of extinction.

The Humane Society of the United States makes a difference in the lives of animals here at home and worldwide. The HSUS is dedicated to creating a world where our relationship with animals is guided by compassion. We seek a truly humane society in which animals are respected for their intrinsic value, and where the human-animal bond is strong.

Want to help animals? We have plenty of suggestions. Adopt a pet from a local shelter, join The Humane Society and be a part of our work to help companion animals and wildlife. You will be funding our educational, legislative, investigative and outreach projects in the U.S. and across the globe.

Or perhaps you'd like to make a memorial donation in honor of a pet, friend or relative? You can through our Kindred Spirits program. And if you'd like to contribute in a more structured way, our Planned Giving Office has suggestions about estate planning, annuities, and even gifts of stock that avoid capital gains taxes.

Maybe you have land that you would like to preserve as a lasting habitat for wildlife. Our Wildlife Land Trust can help you. Perhaps the land you want to share is a backyard— that's enough. Our Urban Wildlife Sanctuary Program will show you how to create a habitat for your wild neighbors.

So you see, it's easy to help animals. And The HSUS is here to help.

THE HUMANE SOCIETY
OF THE UNITED STATES.

2100 L Street NW • Washington, DC 20037 • 202-452-1100
www.hsus.org

ABOUT THE AUTHOR

When her son, Jeffrey, waved good-bye as he headed off to preschool several years ago, Cindy Ferraino started dabbling in newspaper reporting for a local newspaper. Since that time, she has expanded her writing career to include magazine features for national and regional publications, feature articles for websites, ghostwriting for various websites, and stories for books about the joys of parenting multiple birth children.

Before Cindy became a full-time freelance writer, she worked in non-profit grants and accounting administration for a medical school in Philadelphia. Cindy Ferraino is a graduate from Philadelphia University (formerly Philadelphia College of Textiles and Sciences) with a bachelor's degree in accounting.

ACKNOWLEDGEMENTS

To the reader or the person who needs to research a business term — I hope you find what you are looking for and perhaps even more, because this book will help you make sense of all the terms that swirl around the business world.

To the great people at Atlantic Publishing, especially my editor, Shannon McCarthy, for the support and understanding when it came to deadlines and the opportunity to work on a great project.

To my kids, Lyndsey, Erika, and Jeffrey — you are the reason I was able to complete this book during your summer vacation. I am so grateful for your patience when I worked while you waited for food, a ride, and everything in between.

To my husband, Jeff — I can only sum up what I feel about you in a few words: Thank you for everything.

TABLE OF CONTENTS

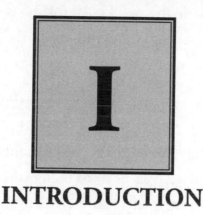

INTRODUCTION

Years ago, individuals who worked in the field of accounting and bookkeeping were called "bean counters." They were put in charge of maintaining fiscal practices of a business or company — counting the beans, so to speak.

Now, the tremendous growth in the accounting and bookkeeping field has changed the "bean counter" role into that of "jack-of-all-business-trades." Individuals, from small business owners or taxpayers to CEOs of major conglomerates, have expanded their accounting and bookkeeping knowledge to include investing, financial, and management terms.

Business professionals, whether they are owners of the local mom-and-pop community food store or a top manager at Campbell Soup Company, have been forced to deal with accounting issues ranging from payroll taxes to the possibility of being accused of fraudulent activity.

General accounting and bookkeeping issues can be handled by individuals or business departments. Balancing a budget, handling problems with health care insurance premiums, or even checking to make sure the petty cash fund has enough money in it are just a few of the duties that fall under the job umbrella for a general accountant or bookkeeper.

Investment accountants are charged with figuring out a profit margin on 20 shares of oil stock or trying to thwart a potential ponzi scheme, while managerial accountants are called in to check on manufacturing plants or to make sure that the company management is dotting their I's and crossing their T's.

Financial accountants are responsible for managing the fiscal practices of companies. These accountants can be part of an in-house or private accounting and auditing department. Their duties include the preparation of financial statements, performing internal audit reviews on departments, and interacting with company personnel.

Because of the diverse nature of accounting and bookkeeping, there is a need for a resource that can help anyone who needs to gain a basic understanding of accounting and bookkeeping or just needs a refresher when it comes to reviewing a financial statement from an investment company. This book will serve as that guide for you; it is designed as Accounting 101, Investing 101, and Management 101 rolled into one informative and engaging tool to be used in class, in the office, or at home.

Designed like a dictionary, the traditional A to Z format of this book is suited to anyone who wants to access information quickly without the hassle of jumping back and forth through a long index of terms. *The Complete Dictionary of Accounting and Bookkeeping Terms Explained Simply* aims to serve as a powerful yet easy-to-understand resource for both the new investor and the seasoned accountant.

The outline of the book is designed to quickly identify the word for which you are seeking a definition. Each section of the outline is broken down in A to Z format. The section on acronyms and abbreviations can be utilized to figure out the description for the most commonly used terminology in business. The acronym and abbreviation list was developed using several current resources available on the market. Because these are acronyms and abbreviations and stand for a specific entity, they cannot be reworded without losing the integrity of the acronym or abbreviation. This author has listed the resources used in the development of this dictionary and gives full credit to the developers of those resources for making this list as complete as possible. The author in no way implies that these acronyms or abbreviations are her own work. This list is not all-inclusive, and not all terms are used in every accounting practice.

When I was in high school, my father gave me an abacus. I guess you could say that my father was sharing his love of accounting with me — or maybe he just liked giving weird gifts. I do not believe my father was trying to plant the accounting seed in me that early; rather, I think he realized that I enjoyed the business courses I was taking at the time.

When I graduated from college, though, I did end up joining my father in his profession. Both my father and I enjoy the challenge of crunching the numbers and balancing the books. But as time has gone on, so too our roles as "bean counters" have changed. We have become jacks-of-all-business-trades, too. My dad has become more involved in specialty-fraud accounting. As for me, I am no longer maintaining budgets for a non-profit medical university. Instead, I am using my accounting knowledge to write.

After countless hours of research, writing, and burning some dinners for my family — they are slowly forgiving me for this one — I am happy to have undertaken this project. Not only did I revive the energy I had when I picked up my first accounting book, but I also learned more about the pulse of the business world as it beats today. I hope you will learn something new too, and perhaps experience for yourself the same passion for numbers that inspired me to join the accounting ranks.

CASE STUDY: WHAT IS FORENSIC ACCOUNTING?

William L. Keenan, CPA
Penn Valley, PA
E-mail: wkeenanl@comcast.net

Employment in public accounting:
20+ years

Forensic accounting is defined as a specialty practice service performed by an individual CPA or within an accounting firm setting by a group or team. Forensic services engagements typically — with respect to the larger U.S. national and regional accounting firms — fall into the category of professional services described as non-audit services or consulting services. Such engagements are most often associated with present or anticipated disputes or litigation. The term "forensic" means suitable or acceptable in court, and accountants practicing in this specialty area, if engaged to give expert testimony, must meet the standard of the court to give expert evidence. The forensic accountant must be prepared to demonstrate and prove to the court that he or she possesses not only the requisite accounting and auditing skills, but also a high level of investigative experience, in order to qualify as an expert on the matter or issue before the court. Quantifying damages and calculating economic losses and investigative findings into alleged malfeasance and fraud are common types of forensic engagements.

Although several different professional organizations confer a special designation to CPAs with experience and training in forensic accounting, the following addresses only the Certified in Financial Forensics (CFF) designation issued by the American Institute of CPAs (AICPA). The credential combines specialized forensic accounting expertise with core knowledge and practice skills relative to the underlying principles of accounting and finance. In addition, the CFF designation encompasses advanced investigative and forensic abilities acquired through actual work experience. This specialty subset of consulting services includes engagements in a variety of service areas such as bankruptcy, insolvency and reorganization, computer forensic analysis, economic damages calculations, family law, fraud prevention and detection, and white-collar criminal investigations involving alleged malfeasance and/or financial statement misrepresentation.

To qualify for the CFF designation, a CPA must be a member in good standing of AICPA, have at least five years of experience in the practice of accounting, and meet minimum requirements with respect to relevant business experience and continuing professional education. Similar designations conferred by other professional organizations include Certified Forensic Accountant (Cr.FA), which applies to the American College of Forensic Examiners International, and Certified Fraud Examiner (CFE), which applies to the Association of Certified Fraud Examiners.

GLOSSARY OF ACRONYMS
AND ABBREVIATIONS

Note: The list serves a guide to understanding the many acronyms and abbreviations you may come across in the different types of accounting practices.

A/C   Account Current

ACRS   Accelerated Cost Recovery System

AAA   Accumulated Adjustments Account

AAA   American Accounting Association

AAA   Association of Accounting Administrators

AADA   Adjusted Attributable Deposit Amount

AAFA   American Association of Finance and Accounting

AAGR   Annual Average Growth Rate

AAI   Accredited Adviser in Insurance

ABC	Activity Based Costing
ABCDS	Asset Backed Credit Default Swap
ABM	Activity Based Management
ABO	Accredited Personal Financial Planning Specialist
ABS	Accounting and Billing System
ABS	Automated Bond System
ACA	Actual Cost Adjustment
ACCS	Advanced Cash Control System
ACCT	Account
ACE	Accumulated Cash Equivalence
ACMB	ABSA Corporate and Merchant Bank
ACP	Annual Compensation Payment
ACPU	Average Cost Per Unit
ACRS	Accelerated Cost Recovery System
ACSEC	Accounting Standards Executive Committee
ACV	Actual Cash Value
ACV	Annualized Contract Value
ACW	ATM Cash Withdrawal
ADA	Average Daily Attendance

ADI	After Date of Invoice
ADJ	Adjust
ADM	Automatic Deposit Machine
ADM	Average Daily Membership
ADP	Average Deferral Percent
ADP	Actual Deferral Percentage
ADR	Asset Depreciation Range
ADR	Average Daily Rate
ADR	Accounting Department Revenue
ADS	Alternative Depreciation System
AE	Actual Expense
AEC	Average Efficiency Cost
AECC	Accounting Education Change Commission
AECS	Audit Engagement Control Sheet
AEI	Average Earnings Index
AEV	Alternative Equivalent Value
AFC	Average Fixed Cost
AFDA	Allowance for Doubtful Accounts
AFDC	Aid to Families with Dependent Children

AFE	Authorization for Expenditure
AFR	Applicable Federal Rate
AFTR	Applicable Federal Tax Rate
AFTS	Automatic Funds Transfer Services
AGI	Adjusted Gross Income
AGM	Adjusted Gross Margin
AGR	Adjusted Gross Revenue
AICPA	American Institute of Certified Public Accountants
AJE	Adjusting Journal Entry
AMT	Alternative Minimum Tax
AMT	Amount
AMTI	Alternative Minimum Taxable Income
AN	Account Number
AP	Accounts Payable
APA	American Payroll Association
APB	Accounting Principles Board
APBI	Accounting Principles Board Interpretations
APBO	Accounting Principles Board Opinions

APBS	Accounting Principles Board Statements
APC	Annual Percentage Change
APC	Actual Payment Coefficient
APD	Actual Profit Difference
APE	Annual Premium Equivalent
API	Accountants for the Public Interest
API	Accountable Property Inventory
APM	Accounts Payable Maintenance
APO	Automatic Payment Order
APR	Automatic Payment Receipt
APR	Annual Percentage Rate
APR	Annual Performance Report
APY	Annual Percentage Yield
AQL	Acceptable Quality Level
AR	Annual Return
ARB	Accounting Research Board
ARM	Adjustable-Rate Mortgage
ARN	Account Reference Number
ARP	Automatic Remittance Processing

ARPU	Average Revenue Per Unit
ARV	Average Retail Value
ARV	Approximate Retail Value
ASB	Accounting Standards Board-British
ASB	Auditing Standards Board
ASBO	Association of School Business Officials
ASCII	American Standard Code for Information Interchange
ASR	Accounting Series Releases
ASWA	American Society of Women Accountants
AT	Automatic Transfer
AT	After Tax
ATB	Accounting Terminology Bulletins
ATC	Average Total Costs
ATM	Automatic Teller Machine
ATO	Asset Turnover
AV	Accepted Value
AV	Actual Value
AVC	Average Variable Costs

AWP	Average Wholesale Price
AWS	Annual Wage Supplement
BA	Banker's Acceptance
BA	Balance Accounting
BAC	Budgeted At Completion
BARS	Budgeting Accounting and Reporting Systems
BAS	Business Activity Statement
BAVL	Budget Availability
BBR	Best Bank Rate
BCD	Balancing Charge Debit
BCE	Balance
BCL	Bank Credit Letter
BD	Bank Draft
BE	Budget Entity
BE	Bill of Exchange
BE	Bill of Entry
BFI	Business Fixed Investment
BFP	Basic Formula Price
BG	Bank Guarantee

BIN	Bank Identification Number
BKPR	Bookkeeper
BL	Bottom Line
BLR	Base Lending Rate
BOA	Bank of America
BOM	Bill of Materials
BOQ	Bill of Quantities
BOS	Bill of Sale
BPI	Building Price Index
BS	Balance Sheet
BTA	Business Travel Allowance
BU	Base Unit
BV	Book Value
C	Credit
C&F	Cost and Freight
CAD	Current Account Deficit
CAFR	Comprehensive Annual Financial Report
CAGR	Compound Annual Growth Rate
CAGR	Cumulative Aggregate Gross Revenue

CAIS	Credit Account Information Sharing
CAP	Customer Approved Payment
CAPEX	Capital Expenditures
CAPM	Capital Asset Pricing Model
CAPS	Corporate Accounts Payable System
CAR	Compounded Annual Rate
CAR	Capital Acquisition Request
CAR	Compound Annual Return
CARR	Compound Annual Rate of Return
CAS	Cost Accounting Standards
CAS	Comprehensive Annual Statement
CAS	Composite Accounting System
CASB	Cost Accounting Standards Board
CAT	Constant Amortized Time
CATS	Customer Account Tracking System
CB	Chargeback
CBA	Centrally Billed Accounts
CBD	Capacity Bonded Debt
CC	Credit Card

CC	Cash Commodity
CCA	Capital Cost Annuity
CCA	Capital Cost Allowance
CCAC	Cash Check and Charge
CCS	Credit Card Status
CCS	Cost of Common Stock
CD	Certificate of Deposit
CD	Cash Disbursement
CDO	Collateral Debt Obligation
CEO	Chief Executive Officer
CF	Cash Flow
CFCT	Cash Flow Cycle Time
CFTC	Commodity Futures Trading Commission
CFM	Certified Financial Manager
CFO	Chief Financial Officer
CFP	Certified Financial Planner
CFPB	Certified Financial Planning Board
CFS	Certified Financial Statements
CFS	Comprehensive Financial Strategies

CGL	Commercial General Liability
CGR	Compound Growth Rate
CI	Compound Interest
CIA	Certified Internal Auditor
CIA	Cash in Advance
CIO	Chief Investment Officer
CIP	Carriage and Insurance Paid
CIP	Central Investment Program
CISA	Certified Information Systems Auditor
CISA	Certified Information Systems Auditor
CIT	Cash in Transit
CMA	Certified Management Accountant
COO	Chief Operating Officer
CPA	Certified Public Accountant
CPI	Consumer Price Index
CSV	Cash Surrender Value
DARTs	Daily Average Revenue Trades
DAC	Deferred Acquisition Costs
DACF	Debit-Adjusted Cash Flow

DASH 401(k) Double Advantage Safe Harbor 401(k)

DAT Direct Access Trading

EBIT Earnings Before Interest and Taxes

EBITDA Earnings Before Interest, Taxes, Depreciation, and Amortization

EBITDAR Earnings Before Interest, Taxes, Depreciation, Amortization, and Rent

EBT Earnings Before Taxes

EC Electronic Commerce

ED Exposure Draft

EDI Electronic Data Interchange

EDP Electronic Data Processing

EITF Emerging Issues Task Force

EFTS Electronic Fund Transfer

EOM End-of-the-Month

EOQ Economic Order Quantity Model

EPS Earnings Per Share

EV Embedded Value

EVA Economic Value Added

FAE	Foundation for Accounting Education
FAF	Freight Analysis Framework
FAS	Financial Accounting Standards
FASB	Financial Accounting Standards Board
FCF	Free Cash Flow
FCFF	Free Cash Flow for the Firm
FCFE	Free Cash Flow to Equity
FGI	Finished Goods Inventory
FICA	Federal Insurance Contributions Act
FIFO	First-In, First-Out Method
FISH	First-In, Still Here
FOB	Free on Board
FOK	Fill or Kill
FMV	Fair Market Value
FTE	Flow Through Equity
FTE	Full Time Equivalent
FUTA	Federal Unemployment Tax
FV	Future Value
GAAP	Generally Accepted Accounting Principles

GAS	Governmental Accounting Standards
GASB	Governmental Accounting Standards Board
GATT	General Agreement on Tariffs and Trades
GDP	Gross Domestic Product
GDI	Gross Domestic Income
GFOA	Government Finance Officers Association
GIPS	Global Investment Performance Standards
GL	General Ledger
GPFS	General Purpose Financial Statements
GRAT	Grantor Retained Annuity Trust
GTM	Good This Month
HERA	Housing and Economic Recovery Act
HFT	High Frequency Trading
HIPAA	Health Insurance Portability and Accountability Act
HLT	High Leveraged Transaction
HOA	Home Owner's Association Fee
HRA	Health Reimbursement Account
HSA	Health Savings Act

HTML	Hypertext Markup Language
HWI	Help-Wanted Index
IAA	Internal Accounting Association
IAFE	International Association of Financial Engineers
IAFP	International Association for Financial Planning
IAG	International Auditing Guidelines
IAI	Independent Accountants International
IAN	Index Amortizing Note
IAPC	International Auditing Practices Committee
IAS	International Accounting Standards
IASC	International Accounting Standards Committee
IB	Introducing Broker
IBES	Institutional Brokers Estimate System
IBF	International Banking Facility
ICFA	Institute of Chartered Financial Analysts
ICFP	Institute for Certified Financial Planners
ICURVE	Interpolated Yield Curve
IDA	Individual Development Act
IFA	International Federation of Accountants

IIA	Institute of Internal Auditors
IMA	Institute of Management Accountants
IPO	Initial Public Offering
IRR	Internal Rate of Return
IRS	Internal Revenue Service
ISP	Internet Service Provider
JAJO	January, April, June, and October
JCP	Junior Capital Pool
JIT	Just-in-Time
JTWROS	Joint Tenant with Right of Survivorship
KIPPERS	Kids in Parents' Pockets Eroding Retirement Savings
LAN	Local Area Network
LCM	Lower Cost of Market
LDR	Loss Disallowance Rule
LGD	Loss Given Default
LIFO	Last-in, First-Out Method
LLC	Limited Liability Company
MAP	Management of an Accounting Practice

MCS	Management Consulting Services
MIS	Management Information System
NAA	National Association of Accountants
NAAI	National Association of Accountants in Insolvencies
NPV	Net Present Value
NRV	Net Realizable Value
NSA	National Society of Accountants
NYSE	New York Stock Exchange
OTC	Over-the-Counter Board
P/E	Price/Earnings
PA	Public Accountant
PEG	PEGY ratio
PERT	Program Evaluation and Review Technique
PFP	Personal Financial Planning
PFS	Personal Financial Specialist
PPBS	Program Planning Budgeting System
POP	Point of Purchase
POS	Point of Sale

QDRO   Qualified Domestic Relation Order

QC   Quality Control

QCP   Quality Control Policies and Procedures

QCS   Statements of Quality Control Standards

QCSI   Interpretations of Quality Control Standards

QR   Quality Review

RAP   Regulatory Accounting Principles

RIA   Registered Investment Adviser

ROA   Return on Total Assets

ROC   Return on Capital

ROI   Return on Investment

ROIC   Return on Invested Capital

ROL   Reduction Option Loan

RONA   Return on Net Assets

SAP   Statements on Auditing Procedure

SAS   Statement of Accounting Standards

SAS   Statements on Auditing Standards

SEC   Securities and Exchange Commission

SFAS	Statements of Financial Accounting Standards
T-BILL	Treasury Bill
TAN	Tax Anticipation Note
TIE	Time Interest Earned
VAT	Value-added Tax
WAC	With Approved Credit
WIP	Work in Process Inventory
YOC	Yield on Cost
YOY	Year over Year
YTC	Yield to Call
YTD	Year to Date
YTM	Yield to Maturity
ZBB	Zero-Base Budgeting
ZEBRA	Zero Basis Risk Swap

CASE STUDY: WHAT IS A CPA?

William L. Keenan, CPA
Penn Valley, PA
E-mail: wkeenanl@comcast.net

Employment in public accounting:
20+ years

As professionals in the areas of business and finance, CPAs fulfill a vital function within our society. Their role is to serve the public interest and maintain public trust. It is expected that in the performance of any service, CPAs will exhibit the highest degree of integrity and objectivity. CPAs handle a variety of jobs and tasks, ranging from basic income tax preparation and advice to rendering an opinion on the representations of management as contained in the financial statements and records they have been engaged to audit.

To become a CPA, the candidates must possess certain minimum qualifications. In most states, they must have 150 hours of college credit (the equivalent of a master's degree) to meet the state's specific minimum licensing requirements. Typically, they must have two years of work experience in public practice and have successfully completed a specific number of credit hours or a specific number of courses at the undergraduate level in accounting and business law, and they must pass a rigorous four part examination. In most states, generally within two or three years after becoming licensed, to maintain their license, CPAs must take 120 hours of continuing education courses every 3 years in order to stay abreast of changes in their profession.

CHAPTER

TYPES OF ACCOUNTING

Accounting: A service activity whose purpose is to provide primarily financial information about economic entities and is intended to make economic decisions.

Accrual accounting: When a company has to account for revenue and expenses even though the payment for products and services has not been rendered.

Behavioral accounting: A type of system that factors in the values of the individuals leading the companies instead of focusing on the actual costs involved in operating the company. This system is often referred to as "human resources accounting."

Black-box accounting: The use of an accounting system that does not represent income and expenses, as with a normal accounting practice. A company looking to bury unwanted financial issues might try to use this type of accounting.

Bookkeeping: The process of recognizing income and expenses on financial statements and ledgers.

Cash-basis accounting: The recognition of revenue when it is deposited and expenses when they actually happen. Small businesses and corporations utilize this method. This is a legal form of accounting and accepted by the Internal Revenue Service (*see Accrual accounting*).

Financial accounting: The act of overseeing the financial operations of companies based on accounting standards.

Forensic accounting: A method of accounting that deals with financial procedures that have been challenged or charged as illegal. One example of forensic accounting is examining insurance fraud claims.

Fund accounting: A type of accounting used by non-profit organizations. This method focuses on how organizations meet their business objectives without a large concern over garnishing a great profit return.

Generational accounting: This type of accounting monitors the present economic status based on previous years to determine how the economy will function in the next generation gap.

Hedge accounting: A type of accounting that involves the treatment of a hedge fund the same as accounting for other investments. The basis behind this accounting method is to utilize only one market value for all investments.

Inflation accounting: An accountant will correct financial statements that were prepared with historical costs and not actual costs.

Managerial accounting: This method of accounting focuses on the management practices of a company. The issues dealing with this type of accounting are manufacturing, costing methods, and budgeting for production.

Not-for-profit accounting: This type of accounting involves non-profit companies like universities, medical institutions, and federal/non-federal government contractors. These entities must adhere to the not-for-profit (NFP) cost accounting standards.

CHAPTER

2

NUMERALS

12B-1 plan: An investment fund that does not have administration fees associated with it to manage the fund. This option is beneficial for investors who have a small amount money to invest but do not want to be saddled with high administrative costs.

Double advantage safe harbor 401(k) (DASH 401k): A retirement plan set up by an employer to help further protect an employee's investments with the padding from an additional savings strategy — a profit share plan.

401(k): A way for individuals to accumulate money to plan for expenses that will come up during retirement, such as a mortgage or a car payment.

401(k) expense-delivery: The amount charged for contributions by employees involved in the management and processing area of the company. This cost is allocated as an operating cost on the revenue sheet.

401(k) expense-selling: The amount charged for contributions by employees involved in the sales area of the company. This cost is allocated as an operating cost on the revenue sheet.

401(k) expense-warehouse: The amount charged for contributions by employees involved in the warehouse operations of the company. This cost is allocated as an operating cost on the revenue sheet.

401(k) payable: The amount the company has to pay for employee contributions. Some companies match 401(k) contributions immediately, and some do so after one year.

529 plan: An investment strategy for individuals who wish to save money for college expenses for their children. Each state has different rules for the plan based on participating schools or colleges.

CHAPTER 3

DEFINITIONS

Abandonment: Surrendering property that is owned or leased voluntarily, when no successor is named to pass the property to. Generally, if someone has prior ownership in the property, it will revert to him or her. If no one had prior ownership in the property, then it will become the property of the state.

Abatement: A levy imposed by the government that is partly or completely canceled.

ABC agreement: A contract between a brokerage firm and an employee. It contains the rights of the firm, described in an A, B, and C outline, when it comes to purchasing a New York Stock Exchange membership for the employee.

ABC method: A strategy to manage inventory in terms relative to their importance. High-dollar items are generally represented as "A's" and lower value items fall into the "B" and "C" categories.

Abeyance: Describes the legal status of real estate titles when lawful ownership of the property is in question and is being determined.

Abnormal spoilage: When a loss of inventory occurs during manufacturing processes. For example, toys that should have been coated with a blue paint instead had red paint applied to them by a factory machine.

Above par: When an investment is selling higher than the current market price.

Above the line deduction: Amounts that can be taken away from the total income recognized for an individual. These amounts include payments made for alimony/child support or costs associated with education.

Absolute advantage: How one company can manufacture or produce a product or service at a fraction of the cost it takes a competitor to manufacture or produce the same product or service.

Absolute priority rule: When a company has to sell shares of stocks or bonds to pay off debt obligations, the first in line to receive retribution is the creditors. The creditors have seniority over the stockholders.

Absorb: To account or designate costs when losses occur.

Absorption costing: Generally, when normal manufacturing costs are considered product costs and included in inventory. Also known as full costing.

Absorption rate: In real estate, an estimated rate in reference to the rate at which the property in question can be sold or leased in a specific area.

Abusive tax shelter: A limited partnership that is believed to be claiming illegal tax deductions, according to the IRS.

Academy of Accounting Historians: An organization run by volunteers that is dedicated to the study of accounting. They traditionally produce the *Accounting Historians Journal*.

Accelerated bookbuild: An offer for a company to purchase stocks or bonds for a short-term investment. This happens when a company cannot obtain funds for investments because of higher debt obligations.

Accelerated cost recovery system (ACRS): Developed by the U.S. Congress in 1981 and changed in 1986 under the auspices of the Tax Reform Act, this procedure utilizes depreciation techniques dealing with cost recovery periods.

Acceptable quality level (AQL): A method to determine the rate of allowed defects in the manufacturing process.

Acceptance sampling: A procedure that comprises statistics used in the quality control environment. A batch of data is tested to determine whether a part of the units being tested has a given attribute that exceeds a certain percentage rate.

Access time: The length of time that a data storage device takes to process and return data from the time of the original request.

Accidental death benefit: The value of an accidental death insurance policy or life insurance policy that is paid to the beneficiary.

Accommodation endorsement: An agreement in writing to be made liable without consideration of an instrument of credit, such as a notes payable, and it is backed by another person or company to strengthen the credit application. For example, when a larger company endorses a note of one of its subsidiaries.

Accommodative monetary policy: A policy by the Federal Reserve that is used to increase the amount of money available for lending by banks.

Account: A relationship between one party and another, typically expressed in money, that shows the effect of a transaction or transactions on a balance sheet or income statement item. One example is a depositor or borrower with a bank.

Account analysis: To determine the accuracy of costs for a company. A cost accountant performs this by assessing variable costs.

Account balance: The net balance of assets and liabilities during an accounting period.

Account executive: A brokerage firm employee who advises clients, takes their orders, and has the legal powers of an agent. Account executives are monitored by the National Association of Securities Dealers.

Account form: A balance sheet in which assets are located to the left and liabilities are located to the right.

Account measurement: This determines values that are measured as dollars or as products.

Account statement: Any transactions and their effects on charges or open account balances during a specified time.

Accountability: A responsibility to perform a specific function by an individual or department.

Accountancy: The business aspect of accounting that is made up of practice, research, and education. It also includes the guidelines that accountants are to follow when performing their tasks.

Accountant in charge: During an audit, this person is generally responsible for overseeing the accounting processes.

Accountant: A person who performs accounting services.

Accountant's letter: This document outlines the company's financial status for the current operating year. It may include recommendations regarding changes to the accounting operations of the company.

Accountant's liability: This is the legal obligation of an accountant who commits fraud or is negligent in the performance of his or her professional duties.

Accountant's responsibility: Ethical obligation of the accountant to the clients he or she provides professional services for.

Accountants for the public interest (API): An organization that provides technical support to organizations like non-profits and is concerned with the public welfare in terms of accounting principles.

Accountants index: A bibliography full of accounting books and articles that pertain to the accounting field and are of interest to accounting professionals.

Accounting: A service activity where the purpose is to provide primarily financial information about economic entities and is intended to make economic decisions.

Accounting change: A change in accounting principles and methods. These changes must be noted in the footnotes, so all users can adjust to these changes on their side. They can also be so significant that a new release of the term may need to be sent out by various organizations such as the Securities and Exchange Commission.

Accounting control: Procedures that are in place to make sure that accuracy in the record keeping functions is maintained.

Accounting convention: A method or procedure that is based on custom and is subject to change as developments arise and can be outdated by the SEC's Accounting Series Release (ASR).

Accounting cushion: The process of overstating an expense provision, the purpose of which is to provide a larger balance in the estimated liability or allowance account so it maximizes the amount of expense for a later period.

Accounting cycle: The steps used in an accounting transaction from the time it occurs to its occurrence on the financial statement sheets.

Accounting earnings: The amount of revenue the company earned for the year.

Accounting entity: A business or other unit that is being accounted for separately. Systems of accounts are maintained for each entity. These can include corporations, trusts, partnerships, and others.

Accounting equation: In the simplest form of accounting, the value of income must equal the value of expenditures.

Accounting error: An accounting-related item is unintentionally misrepresented or is measured inaccurately.

Accounting event: A transaction record is entered into a business's accounting records.

Accounting manual: A book with the policies, procedures, standards, and guidelines for the accountants of an individual proprietorship or company.

Accounting period: When a company uses an appropriate amount of time to file financial statements. The amount of time can be reported as an annual, quarterly, or monthly statement.

Accounting postulate: A premise that accounting principles have been built upon. For example, practicing continuum in management processes is considered an accounting postulate.

Accounting practice: How accountants work to meet the needs of their clients.

Accounting Principles Board (APB): Before it was dissolved in 1973, this group governed the American Institute of Certified

Public Accountants (AICPA). The AICPA is represented by FASB (Financial Accounting Standards Board).

Accounting principles: The rules and guidelines to which accountants must adhere.

Accounting procedure: The methods used in order to analyze and summarize financial data before it is transferred to the financial statement sheet.

Accounting records: Ledgers that are used in recording and maintaining financial data such as receipts, sales, and purchases.

Accounting Research Bulletin (ARB): These documents highlighted accounting principles and practices used by the American Institute of Certified Public Accountants from 1953 to 1959.

Accounting software: Computer programs that are used to maintain accounting information, like QuickBooks and Peachtree.

Accounting Standards Board (ASB): A British and Irish committee that drafts and approves Statements of Standard Accounting Practices. Took over the task from the Accounting Standards Committee (ASC) in 1990.

Accounting standards: The policies that govern an accountant's behavior and conduct in this professional capacity.

Accounting system: The methods and procedures that are used in recording and reporting events and transactions in a formal record.

Accounting valuation: The accurate assessment of assets.

Accounts payable turnover: This measurement determines how payments are made to vendors. The calculation is the amount of purchase divided by the company's total in the accounts payable ledger.

Accounts payable: This amount represents money owed to a company for which a service was rendered. The company records this as a liability until the debt is repaid.

Accounts receivable turnover: This is a rate determined by the time the company will be repaid, either in short or longer terms.

Accounts receivable: Monies owed for goods and services purchased from a company by a customer. They are listed as assets on the balance sheet.

Accredited personal financial planning specialist: This individual helps clients handle management and responsibility of their own financial portfolio. The specialists maintain certification through the Certified Financial Planner Board of Standards (CFPB).

Accretion: The growth that occurs through mergers and acquisitions.

Accrual accounting: When a company has to account for revenue and expenses even though the payment for products and services has not be rendered.

Accrual basis: An alternative to cash basis accounting. This method is utilized when assets and liabilities are valued, but no money has been received by the company.

Accrual bonds: These types of bonds do not make periodic interest payments. They do, however, accrue interest until the bond reaches maturity.

Accrued benefits: Benefits earned by an employee. They are based on years of service to a company and are considered a pension benefit.

Accrued bond: A company will issue this financial instrument to investors who are looking to increase their return without a high risk attached. The interest dividend payment will be issued when the bond matures.

Accrued expense: A cost that has been incurred but does not get recorded in accounting books.

Accrued interest: Interest that has been calculated before the bond is sold.

Accumulated depreciation: The sum of value-loss charges to date on a fixed asset.

Accumulated depreciation — buildings: The cost allocated as an expense for the useful life of a building. This expense can only be taken as long as the company still owns the buildings.

Accumulated depreciation — equipment: The cost allocated as an expense for the useful life of equipment. This expense can only be taken as long as the company still owns the equipment.

Accumulated depreciation — land: The cost allocated as an expense for the useful life of the land. This expense can only be taken as long as the company still owns the land.

Accumulated earnings tax: This tax is enforced only when a company has overstated income and other profits.

Accumulation: The process in compounding cumulative retained profit.

Accuracy: The correctness of an item in accounting.

Acid test ratio: This is derived by dividing the most liquid current assets by current liabilities. See *Quick ratio*.

Acquired surplus: A non-capitalized portion of net worth of a successor company in a pooling of interests combination.

Acquisition cost: The price paid to buy goods and services. It is the list price plus normal incidental costs to acquire an item.

Acquisition: A company that assumes financial and legal responsibilities during a transfer of ownership.

Across the board: In the stock market, this is the movement that affects almost all other stocks that are moving within the same direction.

Active account: An account located at a bank or a brokerage firm in which there are many transactions.

Activities base system: Systematic information that gives quantitative facts about an activity within an organization.

Activity account: The name given for a designated account of activity work performed for a specific area, such as "sanitation and waste collection."

Activity attributes: The general characteristics of an activity.

Activity base: This relates to production activity that is used to demonstrate factory overhead to production.

Activity center: A pool of the cost of two or more activities.

Activity: Actions that consume time and resources, such as manufacturing a new product.

Actuary: A practitioner involved in mathematical computations and analyses of insurance probability estimates.

Ad valorem: Derived from a Latin term that means "according to the value." This is used when applying taxes to goods or property. For example, Georgia has an *ad valorem* tax applied to all vehicle tag renewals. This amount is equal to the assessed price of the vehicle.

Adequate disclosure: This is found in the body of a financial statement. It is a clear and comprehensive disclosure that assists the readers in making proper investment and credit decisions.

Adjudication: When a court rules on a judgment based on a business case. A business case involves charges for bankruptcy or fraud.

Adjunct account: The place where an increased face value of an asset is recorded. An asset that is recorded in this account is considered bonds payable, because this amount increases if the face value of the investment increases.

Adjusted basis: This is used for tax purposes. It is the value used as a beginning point to compute depreciation or gain on the disposition of fixed assets.

Adjusted entries: If changes need to be made on transactions recorded during the accounting year, an entry is made to correct or adjust any income and expenses.

Adjustment bond: A bond issued in exchange for outstanding bonds when recapitalizing a corporation that is facing bankruptcy.

Adjustment date: The effective date of the rate of change on an adjustable-rate mortgage (ARM).

Administration bond: An individual who is handling an estate for a third party will secure a bond to help offset expenses acquired during the processing of the estate.

Administrator: A court-appointed person or bank that is responsible for carrying out a court's decision where the descendants' estate is considered. They oversee this decision as directed by the court until the estate is fully distributed to all the claimants.

Adverse opinion: An auditor's findings report that the company's financial statements do not accurately report the financial status.

Adverse selection: Individuals with significant health issues who file claims in order to get medical insurance.

Advertising costs: Money paid for company or business exposure and marketing.

Advertising sales ratio: The measurement on how efficient a company's marketing strategy is. The ratio is calculated by dividing the number of advertising expenses by the amount of sales for the year. If the number is low, the strategy is working well.

Adviser account: An investment broker will set up this account to help a client with his or her financial needs. This account gives sole rights to the client based on advising from the investment broker.

Adviser fee: The charge for an investment broker who advises his or her clients on high-end mutual funds.

Advisory letter: A newsletter that offers financial advice to its subscribers.

Affidavit: A statement made, both in writing and under oath, before an authorized person such as a judge or a notary.

Affidavit of domicile: A sworn statement that is written by the executor of an estate and certifies the residence of a decedent at the time of his or her death.

Affidavit of loss: A formal document that describes the destruction or deletion of an investment. The document outlines how the investment was destroyed or deleted from the owner's possession, usually through theft or misplacement.

Affidavit of title: During a property transfer, this statement is created to describe the current ownership of the property and how it will be transferred and handled by the new ownership.

Affinity fraud: When an individual or group of people set up bogus investment strategies for investors to take part in. This type of fraud is equivalent to *Pyramid selling.*

After-acquired clause: A mortgage clause agreement that states that any additional property obtained by the borrower after signing the initial contract will be considered subsequent secured property.

After-hours dealing or trading: Stock or bond trading that takes place after business hours on exchanges.

After-tax basis: The basis for comparing returns on corporate taxable bonds and municipal tax-free bonds.

After-tax real rate of return: Revenue that is recognized once taxes have been deducted from the investment.

Aftermarket: Activity of trading that follows immediately after an initial public offering (IPO).

Against actual: An agreement between two investors to obtain the same stock and then eventually sell the stock for cash payments.

Against the box: The sale by the holder of a long position in the same stock.

Aggregate: In a manufacturing process, this term represents the amount of products created in one production cycle.

Aging of accounts: Accounts that are classified when the billing or receivable time has expired.

Aging receivables: Accounts are listed by the dates payment should have been received.

Aging schedule: Classifying trade accounts receivable by date of sale.

Air pocket stock: Stock that falls rapidly, typically in the wake of negative news, such as unexpected poor earnings.

Airport revenue bond: A tax-exempt bond that is issued by a city, county, state, or airport authority and is used to support the expansion and operation of an airport.

Alien corporation: When a company is governed by laws from another country but operates a business within another jurisdiction. For example, an Italy-based olive oil supplier opens a store in New York City.

Alimony payment: Used in divorce as a payment from one spouse to another.

All-purpose financial statement: A statement that covers all the needs of the financial statement users.

Allocate: Spreading and distributing costs over two or more accounting periods that are normally based on fair market values.

Allowance: An acceptable reduction in the quality or quantity of products due to delays from a supplier, like normal spoilage.

Allowance for bad debts: An occurrence that is associated with accounts receivables that are not collected.

Allowance for depreciation: The amount that is taken for the life of the asset.

Allowance for doubtful accounts: The method of reducing uncollected payments on the financial statement.

Allowance method: A way of accounting for bad debts. This method generally is good for matching bad debt expenses against the sales.

Allowance to reduce inventory — LCM (lower cost of market): The method to allocate a credit towards an inventory purchase and a debit against the inventory expense (LCM).

Alternative assets: A valued instrument that is not included on a financial statement. An example of this could be a baseball card collection valued at $5,000.

Alternative minimum tax: A levy created with the purpose of having everyone pay a fair share of tax. President Obama has put a clamp on the use of this method until further discussion about the validity of this tax during current economic conditions.

Altman Z-score: Created by New York University Professor Edward Altman, this method is a valid indicator of bankruptcy. This measures your ability to pay or expect solvency.

American Institute of Certified Public Accountants (AICPA): The governing board that oversees the duties of certified public accountants.

Amortization expense: The cost applied to an asset that involves research contracts or plant rights.

Amortization of bond costs: The allocation of an expense that represents how much interest was gained on the bond note.

Amortization of bond discount: This applies to the interest accrued on the bond and how is should be allocated on the financial statement. This transaction is marked on the right-side column.

Amortization of bond premium: The cost of how much was paid during the life of the bond and where the transaction will be allocated on the financial statement.

Amortization of intangible assets: The recording of these assets from one financial statement to another.

Amortization schedule: For each asset or liability, a separate sheet must show how much cost will be depreciated for the life of the asset or liability. For example, a bond sheet will show how much was depreciated each year on the interest and revenue accrued for the bond.

Amortization: This process evaluates the price of intangible assets of a periodic expense. The price will be reduced over a certain amount of time.

Amortize: Writing off a consistent portion of assets over a set period of time.

Amount realized: Used in the tax area in reference to money obtained or the fair market value of services or property that is received upon a sale or exchange of property.

Analyze: To take an accounting item and evaluate it for possible reasons for discrepancies.

Annual budget: A budget that is prepared to coincide with a calendar or fiscal year.

Annual percentage rate (APR): A cost consumers pay to have credit. Each credit card company develops this rate to attract customers.

Annual report: A corporation's yearly record of its financial condition that is distributed to the shareholders under the Securities and Exchange Commission's regulations.

Annual turnover: The amount of an investment that will carry on to the next year. If the stock has a great rate of return, the annual turnover will be more than a stock with a lesser rate of return.

Annualize: When an item receives an extension from a monthly to a yearly basis.

Annuitant: An individual who received benefits from an annuity.

Annuity due: A form of annuity in which periodic receipts or payments are made at the beginning of the period and one period of the annuity term remains after the last payment.

Annuity in advance: The amount proportioned for each period during the life of an investment.

Annuity in arrears: The amount due for an investment or loan on a set date, like a lease payment on a company-owned vehicle.

Annuity unit: When an individual starts to take payments from his or her retirement accounting but continues to contribute to the fund. An amount will be applied only to what is being withdrawn, and not what is being contributed at that time.

Annuity: A series of equal payments or receipts, such as the interest receipts, on an investment such as a bond.

Antedate: The assignment of a date that is before the date of the original agreement.

Antitrust laws: Federal laws that are created to maintain the status of markets, regulate trade agreements and practices, and provide a competitive market environment.

Any-and-all-bid: An agreement to buy all shares offered for investing during a specified time with a specified price.

Applied costs: A cost that is assigned to a product, department, or activity. An example of an applied cost would be a factory overhead applied to a product.

Applied overhead: Manufacturing costs that are applied to a product and are typically at a predetermined rate.

Appraisal: An estimated value of an asset.

Appraisal capital: This involves writing up an asset when it is appraised at a value that exceeds book value. The entry process is to debit the asset for the new increased value and credit the appraisal capital. Because this can prove to be an inaccurate assessment for capital, this method is rarely used in the United States but may be used in businesses around the world, whereas businesses in the United States appraise capital based an asset's present value.

Appraisal fee: An amount charged by a third party to assess the value of an asset, such as a fee for assessment of a building that is for sale.

Appraisal method of depreciation: A method where the depreciation expense is charged to a certain timeframe that is different when the value of the appraised asset is decreased.

Appreciation: The increased value of an asset.

Appropriated retained earnings: A company will record these amounts in a different account from the originally reported earnings.

Approved list: A list of investments that a mutual fund or other financial institution is authorized to make.

Arbitrage: Profiting from prices when products are divided among different markets.

Arm's length transaction: An exchange between parties who are independent of each other.

Arrears: The amount of money that was never paid to satisfy a loan or other liabilities. Other liabilities include mortgage, tax payment, and lease agreements.

Article of incorporation: This encompasses what a business or corporation does, how they operate, who are the key individuals (owners) or employees of the business or corporation, and out-lines what legal regulations they need to adhere to. The designation is reported within the state where the business or corporation operates.

Asset-conversion loan: When a company is strapped for cash, the company can secure a loan using an asset to pay off short-term debt obligations.

Asset: A profitable benefit for a business or company, like cash.

Asset coverage: Assets that are used to help the company pay for liabilities. This scenario usually happens when a company needs to pay for costs associated with bankruptcy issues. The company can still continue its business operations.

Asset impairment: When a company can no longer use an asset. For example, a piece of equipment used in the manufacturing process has broken to the point that the company is unable to repair or use this equipment. The company can allocate for this loss of equipment in its yearly financial statement.

Asset mix: Proportion of total assets in each asset category.

Asset swapped convertible option transaction (ASCOT): A feature incorporated on a convertible bond that allows the investment to be divided into two parts — a bond and a stock.

Asset turnover: Financial formula that measures how efficient a company is at using its assets to generate sales. It is calculated by dividing sales in dollars by assets in dollars.

Asset/equity ratio: This determines how much revenue a company has. This ratio is calculated by the company's total revenue minus the amount given to stockholders.

Assets: A company's valued products or services.

Assignee: This individual is designated by a business or corporation to help direct specific operations, like an individual who is in charge of life insurance for the company.

Assignment method: To determine how to minimize costs by developing machine workstations.

Assignment method: A problem of determining how to minimize costs by a method of assigning machines and work centers.

Assignment of receivables: Items that have been used to secure a loan.

At par: The price that is the same as the face value, or normal amount, of a security.

At sight: When a bill needs to be paid at the time of service or goods received.

Audit: To assess a company's performance in reference to profit and regulations.

Audit calendar: Specifies when a business or corporation will be evaluated by the government to determine if the accounting practices are in conjunction with the GAAP.

Audit committee: This group enforces the fiscal regulations and responsibilities of corporations that are on an open-exchange market. The committee covers corporations within the United States.

Audit cycle: A period of time in which an accountant conducts audit procedures.

Audit trail: A document to support what has been evaluated for the company.

Audited financial statements: Under the rules of the GAAP, these documents represent what is the financial portrait of a business or corporation.

Auditing evidence: What an auditor uses as proof to substantiate a recorded item so that it can be properly placed as a figure on financial statements. An auditor will check a journal entry for the purchase of equipment on the balance sheet and on the general ledger account.

Auditor: This individual prepares documents to attest to the accuracy and validity of a company's business operations.

Auditor's report: This document must highlight the financial actions of a company based on the principles of the GAAP.

Authorized number of shares of stock: This amount is based on how many shares are offered as publicly traded stock. If the company wishes to issue more shares above the amount approved, the company must receive approval from established stockholders.

Available assets: When a company needs to sell off assets to generate more income. For example: the sale of a property that is no longer useful in the operations of the company.

Average accounting return: The measurement of how much a company will receive back from investments during the fiscal year.

Average accounts receivable: The comparison of how much the company is owed to how many sales the company generated for the accounting period.

Average collection period: The total amount of days from when a transaction was recorded to when money has been received.

Average cost method: An inventory valuation method that is used by assigning the same average cost to each unit sold and to each item in the inventory.

Average cost of inventory: The measurement of how much a piece of inventory is worth in relation to the full amount listed on a company's balance sheet.

Average inventory: The company does an evaluation of how much inventory they started with and what is left during the accounting period. A major factor that will affect this situation is whether the company loses inventory due to a manufacturing or mishandling.

Average payment method: The amount of time a business or corporation has allocated to payment on purchases. The purchases are converted to accounts payable.

Average revenue per unit (ARPU): A business or corporation will receive income based on the sale of one item.

Away from the market: When the purchase price is higher than what the investment is worth on the market.

CHAPTER 4

DEFINITIONS

Baccalaureate bond: An investment strategy that works like a zero-coupon bond that gives individuals the opportunity to put away money for college expenses.

Back door listing: A company that is not registered with the stock exchange and utilizes another company that is listed to sell their stocks on the trading market. This is a legal practice, because some companies do not meet the full requirements to trade but are still allowed to move their stock through another company.

Back pay: This represents payment owed to an individual that falls under terms of a litigation suit. For example, a workers' compensation claim against an employer for loss of wages.

Backlog: When a company has too many unsold goods or services that must be carried over into the next year.

Bad debt: When a payment needs to be collected, but the company knows there is a possibility of having to report a loss on this transaction.

Bad debt expense: This transaction allocates the cost of not receiving payment against expected income.

Bad debt reserve: A company will set up a separate account to support the accrual of lost payments.

Bag holder: A slang term used to describe an investor who holds onto a stock or bond that has little or no value.

Bagel land: A slang term used to describe a stock or bond that is going to hit the bottom of the market with less than a dollar value. Investors try to hold onto the stocks or bonds to see if the market will pick up, but most often these stocks or bonds become worthless.

Bailout: To help a business or corporation get out from underneath bad debts, like if the government were to help out Fannie Mae or Freddie Mac.

Bait and switch: A selfish marketing strategy used to lure consumers into purchasing products or services by offering one product but then changing to a more high-end product once the consumer agrees to make a purchase.

Balance: Positive or negative amounts that are at the bottom of financial statements.

Balance per bank: The total amount that appears on a statement from a financial institution.

Balance per books: The total amount that appears on a company's balance sheet.

Balance sheet account: This area refers to where the total amount of the balance sheet is on a financial statement.

Balance sheet: This statement is used to highlight operations of a business. The statement includes income and expenses.

Balanced budget: When the profit exceeds the amount of liabilities, the company is said to have a bottom line that is profitable and balanced.

Balloon loan: A loan that does not have an amortization schedule so the payoff is higher when the loan reaches term.

Bank endorsement: An individual will authorize payment to an unknown party. The most common is writing a check endorsed with the word "cash" on it.

Bank errors: The accountants' or bookkeepers' responsibility to check bank statements thoroughly to report any mistakes between the financial institution and the company's financial records. By not reporting any discrepancies, the company could stand to lose money in unnecessary fees and transactions.

Bank overdraft: When an individual or company takes out more from an account and the balance drops below the allowed amount by the financial institution.

Bank reconciliation: This method occurs when there are differences in transactions between the bank and company's records.

Bank service charge: Fees charged by a financial institution for servicing and maintaining a depositor's account.

Bank statement: A timeline of the transactions that affect an individual or business account.

Banking book: A register that includes both deposits and withdrawals. This document can be checked against the bank statement to see if the transactions are correct.

Bargain purchase option: A provision of a lease that will allow for the purchase of leased assets in the future by the person leasing it (lessee), and at a set price that is usually so low that the lessee is almost guaranteed to use this option.

Basic accounting equation: The relationship between income, expenses, and the ownership of the company. Income should equal the amount of expenses plus what the owner puts up for the business.

Basket purchase: A lump sum purchase of a number of assets.

Batch size: The evaluation of how many products should be produced for an inventory analysis.

Batch-level activities: The quantity of products produced in one process setting.

Batch-level cost: The allocation of a price for the number of units produced.

Bearer bonds: Bonds in which ownership is determined by possession and for which interest is paid to the holder of the bond.

Bear market: This term refers to the status of the trading market when investments prices are at a low and investors are not comfortable with investing until the market moves upward.

Before reimbursement expense ratio: How much an investment fund is worth until fee payments for fund managers are calculated from the income recognized on the investment.

Beginning inventory: Products or services that a business starts with during a new fiscal year.

Behavioral accounting: A type of system that factors in the values of the individuals leading the companies instead of focusing on the actual costs involved in operating the company. This system is often referred to as "human resources accounting."

Below cost: The recognition of a price expense when it has been incurred. This expense does not get recorded until payment has been recorded.

Below par: When the face value of a stock or bond is lower than the current value of the stock or bond on the trading market.

Below the line: Transactions not considered as part of the year-end financial statement. These transactions will be recognized for the following year.

Benchmark: The comparison of one product to another to evaluate the quality of products being manufactured by a company.

Bequest: In regards to a will or an estate, this term refers to a deceased individual leaving assets to family members or persons closely involved with the deceased individual.

Berry ratio: This method is used to determine a company's financial status at any time during the current fiscal period. The ratio is determined by taking the gross income over the amount of operational costs.

Best ask: The lowest price at which a bid can be recorded.

Best of breed: Like the "best in show" award at a dog show, this term refers to the high quality of stocks or bonds offered during a time when the trading market is at a low point.

Betterments: Asset changes that are designed to provide increases and improvements in services.

Bidding war: When two or more individuals or groups are going after the same product, service, or even real estate property and are willing to pay more to retain a competitive edge.

Bill and hold: When a vendor enters into a purchase agreement with a consumer but does not hand over the product or service after a certain date.

Bill of materials: A compilation of the supplies to be used in manufacturing a product, good, or service.

Billing cycle: The average time set by a business or company when payment should be received. Each business or company will set its own payment schedule.

Bird dog: In real estate, this term refers to investors who search for properties to buy with the intent to purchase but may not initiate a purchase agreement.

Biweekly: To receive or render services twice in one month.

Black ink: This represents a business or company reporting an increase in the amount of revenue on the balance sheet.

Black-box accounting: The use of an accounting system that does not represent income and expenses as with a normal accounting practice. A company looking to bury unwanted financial issues may try to use this type of accounting.

Black market: When individuals or companies try to sell or purchase investments, products, or services that have been illegally acquired.

Blend fund: An investment that has a combination of different funds to yield a higher return.

Blind brokering: When an investment firm does not disclose the information about transactions that happen between buyers and sellers. This is a legal form of an investment transaction.

Blind entries: Often used in general bookkeeping practices, this is an easy way to keep track of income or expenses. This legal form of bookkeeping is utilized by small businesses.

Bloodletting: When an investor suffers a chain of bad investment deals.

Blue-chip stock: Securities issued by companies that have been rated as fiscally responsible and stable entities.

Blue chip: A company that has been rated as a fiscally responsible and stable entity.

Board of directors: Individuals chosen by shareholders of a company to regulate actions made by employees and decision makers.

Bogey: A slang term that refers to how well an investment is performing. Stock analysts commonly use the "S&P 500 index" to figure out the bogey on an investment fund.

Bond: This is a financing vehicle made available by companies to help investors enter into the bond market.

Bond cash price: The shareholder will purchase the bond at a set price.

Bond certificate: A certificate of indebtedness that is issued by a company or government agency that guarantees payments of a principal at a specified time frame plus periodic interest.

Bond coupon rate: The amount of interest reported on a bond.

Bond discount: When a bond is sold below its face value, the price of a bond is compared to the face value of the bond.

Bond fund: When a mutual fund decides to open a new bond.

Bond indenture: A contract between the issuing entity and the bondholder. It specifies the terms, rights, and obligations of the contracting parties.

Bond interest expense: The amount recorded as payment received on bonds that reach maturity.

Bond issue cost expense: The record on a financial statement of bonds issued by the company.

Bond issue costs: The expenses associated with bond issues, like maintenance account fees.

Bond premium: When the bond is sold above its face value, the price of the bond is compared to the face value of the bond.

Bond refinancing: The issuance of new bonds to replace outstanding bonds, either at maturity or prior to maturity.

Bond sinking fund: When a bondholder is close to defaulting on the bond, the company will buy the bond back to avoid further debt incurring on the security.

Bonds payable: The amount due on a bond when it reaches the maturity date. This transaction is recorded as a credit on the balance sheet.

Bonus issue: In lieu of paying out a higher dividend payment, a company may offer more shares of stock to investors.

Book depreciation: The difference between the amount of book value for an asset and how much depreciation is assessed on the asset.

Book inventory: The amount of inventory recorded that is presently in stock.

Book of original entry: The first area where income and expenses are listed before transferring these costs to the proper ledger accounts.

Book profit: The amount recorded when a company issues a bond based on the bond's current face value.

Book to market ratio: The calculation of the amount a company is worth to the amount the company's shares are worth on the trading floor.

Book value of an asset: The amount at which an asset is valued on a company's financial statements.

Book value per share: The difference between the total amount of company shares issued and the amount of shares owned by the company.

Book value: The amount a company has in securities.

Book-to-bill ratio: In cost accounting, this method refers to the comparison of how many products are manufactured to how many products have been sold.

Bookkeeping: To recognize income and expenses on financial statements and ledgers.

Bottom line: The tally of income and expenses. If the amount of income is greater than expenses, the company will report a profit. Conversely, if the amount of expenses is greater than the amount of income then the company will report a loss.

Bounced check: A payment that has been stopped because there is no money available in the account.

Break-even analysis: A method of determining how much profit versus how many expenses will keep a company viable.

Break-even point: The line where a company decides how much income is needed to maintain current operating expenses, when a company reaches an equal amount of recorded income and expenses.

Brochure rule: Under the auspices of the Investment Adviser Act of 1940, investment brokers must inform their clients about changes to their investment policies during the term life of the investment.

Brokerage: An investment broker who charges a fee to secure investments for clients; also used to refer to the business of a broker.

Budget: A document outlining the revenue and expenses for an individual (personal use), business, or corporation.

Budget deficit: When the amount of expenses exceeds the amount of revenue, a company will report a decrease on the financial statements.

Budget surplus: When the amount of revenue exceeds the amount of expenses, a company will report an increase on the financial statements.

Budget variance: The difference in the amount on a current budget to the amount on a projected budget.

Budgetary control: A company plan to effectively measure the relationship between profit and expenses.

Bull market: This term refers to the status of the trading market when investment prices are at a high and investors are comfortable with investing in the market.

Bullet bond: An investment that pays out one payment on the date the investment reaches maturity.

Bunny bond: An investment that enables investors to recycle dividend payments to secure another investment.

Burn rate: When a company starts a new business venture, there is an analysis of how long it will take the company to expend the initial funds.

Business (source) document: A record of business used as the basis to analyze and record transactions. Some examples of this are check stubs, receipts, and invoices.

Business combination: Two businesses are combined successfully through a cash or stock exchange.

Butterfly spread: A combination of investments acquired during a bull and bear market trend. The formation of these investments initiates three different option costs — two are evaluated at the bull price and one is evaluated at the bear price.

Buy: The act of acquiring a product, service, or investment.

Bypass trust: An agreement set up to shelter surviving members of a family from paying a higher estate tax on assets left by a deceased individual. The most common form of this type of trust occurs when the recipients of the estate are minors.

CHAPTER 5

DEFINITIONS

C-share: A type of investment fund that does not carry a high payment load schedule.

Calendar year: Unlike the regular 365 days a year, businesses and corporations operate on a different system instituted by the Internal Revenue Service. This date can be given at any time and run for a 12-month period. For example: A non-profit organization may run from July 1 through June 30th.

Call option: A buyer can utilize his or her contractual rights to obtain shares at a determined price.

Call premium: (1) The amount of the stock that is higher than the par value, or (2) the price an investor has to pay to the writer of the investment.

Call price: Referred to as the *Redemption price.*

Callable: When a company decides to redeem or cancel a security. An example would be a bond or a preferred stock.

Callable bonds: If a company decides to repurchase a bond before the issue reaches maturity.

Callable preferred stock: The situation in which a stockholder has the option to turn in the stock for any price at any time.

Canary call: When a low load bond reaches maturity, this type of bond cannot be utilized to purchase another investment.

Cancelled check: When the payment has already been satisfied and the instrument is no longer valid.

Capital: What a company holds in assets. The assets include money, securities, equipment, and real estate.

Capital appreciation: This represents how much a stock or bond is worth.

Capital asset: A valued instrument used in the day-to-day functions of the company.

Capital budgeting: The determination of how much manufacturing equipment needs to be utilized by the company.

Capital efficiency: The relationship between how many expenses are incurred by the company to how much money is used to manufacture a good or service.

Capital employed: The determination of how much revenue it will cost to produce or manufacture quality products or services.

Capital expenditures (CAPEX): A company will acquire new equipment to use for future manufacturing purposes in order to increase profit margins. For example, buying a parcel of land to construct an addition to the current building. This addition will increase the area of the manufacturing process that in turn will increase production.

Capital growth: To assign assets with securities that will produce a larger profit return.

Capital intensive: Describes a company that acquires an overload of materials to manufacture a product or service.

For example, a trucking company will purchase more trucks to increase freight line productivity.

Capital investment: A valued instrument that maintains a high degree of service for the company.

Capital lease: A lease that is equal financially to the purchase of an asset that is leased.

Capital liability: Expenditures that are classified for a specific use, like research and development for a new product.

Capital loss: The recognition of debt on an asset that is currently valued at less than what the original price was.

Capital maintenance approach to net income: The determination of how much revenue is calculated from one accounting period to the next. For example, if a company reported revenue at $1 million then achieved another $3 million during the accounting period, the total for the next year would be $4 million.

Capital net worth: The difference between the amount of revenue to the amount of expenses.

Capital rationing: A company's ability to watch the acquisition of new securities and other assets, such as real estate. By doing this, a company can increase the viability of current investments held before acquiring new securities.

Capital resource: See *Capital asset.*

Capital stock: Company shareholders will initiate stock issues that are listed on the company's financial statements.

Capitalize: To account for the price of a valued instrument, like the price of equipment.

Capitalized cost: The amount calculated on a lease agreement. This amount includes payment of taxes.

Capitalized interest: Interest that incurs during the self-construction of an asset that is considered to be part of the asset's cost.

Capped fund: A type of investment that puts a limit on the amount of administrative fees that can be charged during the life of the investment.

Carrying amount: Also referred to as *Book value*.

Carrying cost of inventory: This amount relates to the price of how much inventory is currently held in stock. The company uses this number to see how much profit can be realized on the current inventory and how much more should be produced or manufactured to maintain income and expenses.

Carrying value: Also referred to as *Carrying amount*.

Carve-out: Income earned on investments by a parent company that is transferred to another company for ownership rights on the sale of the parent company's subsidiary.

Case study: An evaluation of how an individual, business, or corporation operates in relation to other groups in the same field of operation.

Cash: Currency, coins, and bank deposits recorded by a company.

Cash account: This ledger shows how much cash the company holds.

Cash and cash equivalents: A document that shows how much cash and securities the company holds.

Cash asset ratio: The comparison of a company's income and expenses to determine the viability of a company.

Cash basis: This method is used in bookkeeping to measure how much income is coming in versus how many expenses are incurred.

Cash basis accounting: The recognition of revenue when it is deposited and expenses when they actually happen. Small businesses and corporations utilize this method. This is a legal form of accounting and accepted by the Internal Revenue Service (see *Accrual accounting*).

Cash book: A book in which a business or corporation will record when cash has been received or used as payments for operating expenses.

Cash budget: The amount of cash and securities on a financial statement.

Cash collections: The ability to keep track of payments and receipts of cash and securities.

Cash control: The tracking of cash as income and cash used to pay for expenses.

Cash conversion cycle: The determination of how long a company will stay afloat while waiting to record a profit from sales.

Cash cost: When a company sells a stock or bond to raise quick revenue.

Cash cycle: Also referred to as *Cash conversion cycle*.

Cash discount: By reducing the sales price of a product or service, consumers receive a reduction and the company records a timely payment.

Cash dividends: Payment for supplemental income made on investments in cash form.

Cash earnings: The amount of profit that is recognized after expenses have been deducted.

Cash equivalence: The price a company records on a ledger when a customer has purchased a valued instrument.

Cash flow: The recognition of cash as income and cash used to pay for expenses.

Cash flow after interest and taxes: The amount of cash and securities the company has recorded once interest and tax payments are recognized on a financial statement.

Cash flow from financing activities: This amount represents how much cash has been reported from financial situations like mortgages and bond issues.

Cash flow from investing activities: This amount represents how much cash has been reported on investments and securities.

Cash flow from operating activities: This amount represents how much cash has been reported from day to day business operations of the company.

Cash flow per share: The amount of cash on hand by a company after the issuance of bonds and stocks.

Cash flow statement: A document that reflects how cash was reported as income and how much cash was used to pay for operating expenses.

Cash interest: The amount included in a loan payment.

Cash journal: The area where cash transactions are allocated either as a debit or credit.

Cash management journal: Financial institutions will offer this service to businesses or corporations to help manage income and expenses properly.

Cash method: An accounting method where all the costs are charged to an expense as it is incurred, and revenue is acknowledged as collections are made.

Cash method of accounting: Also referred to as *Cash basis accounting.*

Cash on cash return: The difference between how much cash will be recorded as revenue to how much cash will be needed to pay for expenses.

Cash overdraft: A cash account with a credit balance. For example, $50 in cash was deposited, but the check was written for $100. The difference is reported as a liability on the balance sheet.

Cash payment to suppliers: Payment made for the purchase of goods or services.

Cash pooling: In order for a company to remain solvent, a company may combine cash and securities to avoid costly damages.

Cash ratio: The determination to find out if a company has enough cash to pay off debts quickly.

Cash realizable value: Also referred to as *Net realizable value.*

Cash receipt: The record when a cash payment has been allocated for the sale of a product.

Cash short and over: When there is a discrepancy between cash on hand to cash given out, the amount is recorded in this account on the ledger.

Cash surrender value (CSV): The amount of money given to an insured individual when the policy has stopped or if the policy had reached the maturity time period. This value is usually included in policies that are deemed permanent.

Cash taxes: Payments of cash to satisfy tax assessments.

Cash wages: Payment of salaries made in the form of cash.

Cashier's check: An endorsement that will be paid directly by a financial institution instead of waiting for a payment from a direct banking account. Most companies require a cashier's check, because it is a better guarantee of receiving payment.

Cats and dogs: In financial and investment accounting, this interesting analogy refers to the unusual nature of stocks and bonds that have bounced around the stock market. "Cats and Dogs" stocks are seen when a company is in the first year of business.

Ceiling: The net realizable that is used as an upper limit on the defining market when determining the value of inventory at a lower cost or market.

Certified financial statements (CFS): A document outlining a company's financial activities that has been prepared by a Certified Public Accountant. This document follows rules set by the GAAP.

Certified management accountant (CMA): An accredited professional who handles all aspects of management accounting. Management accounting includes cost analysis, economic forecasting, and quality control.

Certified public accountant (CPA): An accredited professional who handles all aspects of public and private accounting. A CPA performs many accounting duties, including balance sheets, income and expense statements, and profit and loss analysis.

Certitude: The determination that an action is accurate and correct.

Cessation: When a company stops business operations.

Change in accounting estimate: If there is a difference in a depreciation cost, a notation is made in the financial statement.

This affects depreciation expenses. This serves as a proper notification to company personnel and investors.

Change in accounting principles: If a new guideline has been instituted for accounting practices and procedures, a company will make a notation on the financial statement to reflect how an entry was adjusted according to the new ruling. This serves as a proper notification to company personnel and investors.

Charge-off: When a company takes off unpaid receivables from a financial statement. Because this is not reflected on the financial statement, the company must still report the loss of profit.

Charge: A price allocated to a product or service.

Charitable contribution: Businesses that give donations to companies that raise income for other non-profit organizations.

Chart of accounts: A document containing all of the financial accounts of a business or corporation.

Check printing charges: It represents the fee imposed for placing on order for company checks. This expense is reported on a company's balance sheet.

Cherry picking: (1) When investors utilize well-performing investments again for another investment strategy in hopes that the investments will continue to be successful on the market, or (2) the process in which bankrupt companies have favorable contracts upheld by the bankruptcy court but unfavorable contracts are annulled.

Chief executive officer (CEO): The head of a business or corporation that oversees the total functions of the organization. This individual is responsible for providing information to the company's board.

Chief financial officer (CFO): This individual oversees the fiscal operations of a business or corporation.

Chief operating officer (COO): This individual is responsible for overseeing the operational functions of a business or corporation.

Churn rate: The number of consumers who decline subscribed services, like the cancellation of a cell phone plan because another provider has offered a more competitive and lower price.

Classification of assets: Grouping similar assets together to assess a company's performance.

Classified balance sheet: Grouping similar assets and liabilities together to combine the total number of assets and liabilities on one balance sheet.

Clean your skirts: A slang term to describe how an investment broker should make sure the client's best interests are met in acquiring quality investments.

Clear: To balance each account down to zero.

Clearing account: When an account reflects a zero balance.

Closely held account: A business or corporation owned by a few people that utilize this method for investments and securities.

Closing entry: A method used in bookkeeping to close out an account and begin a new account for the next accounting period.

Cloud on title: When a title search is performed for real estate or investment transactions, there may be findings regarding tax or bankruptcy issues. These issues can prevent or "cloud" a title from being processed.

CMA exam: This test is administered to individuals who are seeking to become a Certified Management Accountant. The rules and regulations of this test are governed by each state.

Coefficient of correlation: A balance must be coherent with matching positive number to a negative number.

Coefficient of determination: In cost accounting, this method projects values for the next phase of a project.

Collection agency: An organization that is used to retrieve money that is owed to a business or corporation.

Collection ratio: The method of determining how much money will be collected in a certain time period.

Combined financial statement: These documents are used when a company operates different pieces of the organization that have independent governing bodies — for example, when a medical university is affiliated with a research and development company. The documents are prepared under the GAAP guidelines.

Combined ratio: This method is used for insurance companies to assess how well a company has been performing against competitors. If the company reports a ratio which is less than 100 percent, the company has proved it is earning a profit. Anything above 100 percent puts the company in a bad position because that means the company is paying more in expenses without an increase in revenue.

Comfort letter: This is a safety net for companies that is used to project a good financial position for shareholders.

Commercial year: Unlike a regular calendar year, this method is used to determine how to plan for the next year based on costs incurred in the current year.

Commissions expense: An amount paid to an investment adviser for securing a stock or bond.

Commitment accounting: This method of accounting utilizes the ability to post expenses to accounts even though money has not been paid for products or services purchased. Hiring a caterer for an event a few weeks before the event date would be an example.

Common costs: A price related to several different assets.

Common equity: This amount represents the investment a shareholder has in a company.

Common stock: The shares the company has to offer for investments.

Common stock account: Where the amount of shares issued to shareholders is recorded.

Common stock dividend distributable: A payment to be made to stockholders but it has not been released by the company.

Common-size balance sheet: This document highlights balance sheet accounts in the form of a percentage and not a dollar amount.

Common-size financial statement: This document highlights financial statement accounts in the form of a percentage and not a dollar amount.

Common-size income statement: This document highlights income accounts in the form of a percentage and not a dollar amount.

Common-size statement: This document highlights income and expense accounts in the form of a percentage and not a dollar amount.

Comparability: The act of placing or relating value to similar assets or liabilities.

Comparative financial statements: A company will look over current financial statements and prior year statements to analyze how well the company has performed.

Compensated absences: The authorization of payment for employees who have taken vacations or leaves of absence due to personal reasons. This is governed by accounting standards and guidelines.

Compensating balances: A financial institutions can use money to pay for an outstanding loan.

Completion bond: An investment fund set up for individuals or corporations that have set schedules to finish projects but may not have enough funds to see the projects to the end. This type of bond is common practice with building and entertainment industries that are based on production schedules.

Complex capital structure: A company that has a mixture of stocks and bonds to exchange into common stock.

Compound annual growth rate (CAGR): The amount an investment continues to increase over a set time period.

Compound entry: When an income and expense must be recorded for the same transaction.

Compound interest: The amount of interest calculated on top of the initial loan amount.

Compounding: When an investor gains more interest on an investment that has already received interest payments.

Compounding frequency: The time periods when interest will be calculated on top of the original loan amount.

Compounding period: The length of time from one interest payment to the next.

Comprehensive income: Income that has been recognized after economic changes have been deducted. For example, after a company reports a loss, the loss is deducted from the revenue.

Comps: When a company compares revenue and expenses from the current year to revenue and expenses from a prior year to project future sales margins.

Comptroller: This individual is responsible for the management of the accounting functions for a business or corporation.

Conceptual framework: This falls under the Financial Accounting Standards Board (FASB) ruling in 1998. The ruling involves considerations of how to handle the management when an employee exercises stock option rights.

Concession: The ability for a company to have the main parent company be in one location and a subsidiary to in another location.

Condensed financial statements: Documents with a shortened version of all of the company's financial statements.

Conflict of interest: A situation where someone who must act in an official capacity stands to profit personally from the decision; in such a case, this person must step down from his or her role.

Conservatism: The belief that business systems should follow a safe approach to business practices.

Consigned goods: When products or services are resold by a third party. For example, giving clothes to a consignment shop for resale.

Consignee: The individual who is responsible for a bill of laden, which represents what items will be delivered according to a sale agreement.

Consignment: To sell goods or services for another individual.

Consignor: The individual who provides products or services to another individual.

Consistency: To maintain accuracy of financial statements for future accounting periods.

Constant-dollar: The determination of how the value of the dollar will perform from one year to the next.

Constraints: Describes an accounting method based on the principles of conservation and safe economical trends.

Consumer price index (CPI): The cost consumers will pay for goods or services. This number is changed by rates of inflation.

Contingency fund: This account is used to pay for expenses that incur quickly and were unplanned by the company.

Contingent gain: An unexpected influx of revenue as a result of a litigation suit or real estate sales.

Contingent liability: When the security reaches maturity, the shareholder will receive a discounted dividend if the issuer cannot repay the loan.

Contingent loss: An unexpected decrease in revenue as a result of litigation or real estate sales.

Continuing operations: The process of maintaining day-to-day activities for the current business year and future years.

Continuous inventory: A computerized record of the amount of inventory in stock.

Contra account: The matching of a related debit to a related credit.

Contra asset account: This record will carry a zero amount.

Contra equity account: This amount is represented as a debit for stockholder ownership.

Contra liability account: This amount is represented as a debit.

Contra owner's equity account: Also referred to as *Contra equity account.*

Contra revenue account: This record reflects a decreased balance on reported revenue for the company.

Contributed capital: See *Paid-in capital.*

Contribution approach income statement: This document highlights production costs as they relate to the cost of manufacturing a product and the sale of the product.

Contribution margin rate: The relationship between how much it costs to manufacture a product to how many products were sold at a specific price.

Control account: The balances of assets and liabilities are recorded in this account.

Controller: See *Comptroller.*

Conversion costs: The price of transferring a piece of equipment from one production line to a different section of the manufacturing plant.

Convertible bonds: When the market price remains high, investors can transfer the stock to a bond. The stock must be rated on the current value of the bond.

Convertible preferred stock: Stockholders have the ability to transfer shares to common stock.

Cookie jar accounting: This method utilizes figures from prior years to produce a healthier financial outlook for a company. This method is an unfavorable form of accounting.

Cooking the books: When a company will alter their financial records to project the company's financial status in a profitable way.

Copyright: Laws set forth for an inventor to retain ownership of a product or service. This term also applies to business professionals, writers, and artists.

Corporate cannibalism: A company that tries to saturate an already successful market with the same product or service.

Corporate finance: The area that involves the financial aspects of a business or corporation. Financial aspects include accounting and investments.

Corporation: The formation of a business entity that provides a product or service to consumers. Entities are governed by rules and regulations set forth by state and federal agencies.

Correcting entry: See *Adjusted entries.*

Correlation: Accounting entries must have a specific relationship. For example, the purchase of a piece of equipment must have a corresponding debit and credit journal entry.

Cost accounting: The method by which a business or corporation evaluates the financial operations of the entity in relations to fixed prices and productivity.

Cost flow assumption: Evaluates the LIFO (Last-In, First-Out) or FIFO (First-In, First-Out) methods of calculating inventory.

Cost method of recording treasury stock: In this manor, the purchase of treasury stock is listed on a specific financial statement as a debit entry.

Cost of capital: This relates to how much liquidity a business or corporation has in held investments.

Cost of goods available for sale: The absolute amount of products or services that a business or corporation can possibly sell in a specific time period, usually during a fiscal year.

Cost of goods purchased: The price of products or services that are available for purchase by suppliers or consumers.

Cost of goods sold: The direct cost of the production of products or services that were purchased by consumers.

Cost of sales: See *Cost of goods available for sale*. This is also referred to as the *Cost of goods sold*.

Cost principle: When transactions are recognized for their cost instead of price during the life of the income or expense.

Cost ratio: A method to determine how well a business or corporation handles the management of profits and costs.

Cost structure: A method to determine how much it will cost a company to manufacture a product and how much profit will be recognized from manufacturing the product.

Cost-benefit analysis: The ability to assess how much a project will cost to operate and how much profit the company will gain in production of the project.

Cost-plus pricing: The process of increasing a product price once manufacturing prices have been reached.

Cost: How much a consumer will have to pay for a product or service or how much it will be for a company to manufacture a product.

Costing system: A watchdog to keep company expenses in line with company profits. This system can be done on the computer or by hand in the form of spreadsheets.

Country basket: An investment created to be similar to one that can be traded on an international market.

Coverage ratio: The method to evaluate the financial operations to ensure the company is able to meet debt requirements.

CPA exam: This test is mandated by each state to ensure an individual's authority to become a certified public accountant. In addition to the examination, the candidate must meet certain educational requirements.

Credit balance: This process involves the work of a short sale. Within the short sale, the amount recognized as a profit on the sale is recorded as a credit on a company's general ledger.

Credit line: See *Line of credit*.

Credit order: When a purchase has been made, but payment has not been received or recorded.

Credit sales: Purchases made by a consumer that do not require a payment made in full at the time of purchase.

Credit terms: The length of time a consumer has to repay the amount of debt owed on an obligation. This can also include interest payments.

Credit watch: The ability for an individual, business, or corporation to obtain credit based on a rating by a credit bureau.

Credit: On the balance sheet, this represents transactions recorded in the left column.

Creditor: When payment for goods or services is owed to another individual, business, or corporation.

Cross-holdings: If a business or corporation includes investments held by other companies on their financial statements. This is a legal form of business.

Crossfoot: To summarize ledger accounts going from side-to-side instead of up-to-down.

Crossover rate: When a company works on different product lines, but the lines maintain the same outcome and the same profit margin. For example, a company that manufactures two different washers but still achieves the same quality service and profitability.

Cumulative effect of a change in accounting principle: This falls under FASB. This applies to assets and liabilities that are reported as appreciation or deprecation. The change must be made in the current period.

Cumulative preferred stock: An investment that did not receive certain payment dividends. The dividends have to be given to preferred stockholders before the rest of the remaining shareholders.

Cumulative total return: The amount of profit recognized through the investment period.

Cumulative transition adjustment account: Under FASB guidelines, this appropriation calculates any profit or loss that was accrued throughout the several accounting periods.

Cumulative: The repetition of numbers in sequence. This term is used in cost and managerial accounting.

Current assets: Accounts that are considered to be cash equivalents if a company needs to use them for liquidity, like investments, equipment, and expense accounts (includes rentals).

Current capital: See *Net current assets.*

Current cash debt coverage: The measurement of how a company can convert cash to cover liabilities. The calculation includes taking the actual amount of operating expenses over the actual amount of cash on hand.

Current debt: An obligation that is due one year from the date it has occurred. For example, giving a consumer one year to pay for furniture.

Current liabilities: Accounts on a company's general ledger that must be paid in full for the following year, like accounts payable and term loans.

Current maturity of long-term debt: The amount of money to be received after obligations have been paid towards the principal amount on the loan.

Current portion of long-term debt: See *Current maturity of long-term debt.*

Current ratio: Also referred to as *Cost ratio.*

Current value: To assign a real cost to current assets and expenses.

Current year's net income: This refers to what is currently held as profit earned during the current accounting period.

Curtailment: When a company outsources or sells off a portion of the business operations in order to maintain profitability.

Cushion bond: A type of investment that is sold when the market rates are higher than the current premium rate of the bond.

Custodial account: An account set up at a financial institution or with an investment brokerage to hold savings for a minor until that individual reaches the age of 18.

Customer deposits: An acceptance of payment from a consumer before work has taken place. For example, a disc jockey will take a deposit to hold a date for a customer.

Cut-off point: In reference to a budget principal, this term refers to the level of profit that will be expected on a security.

Cutting the melon: A slang term that refers to when a company issues another dividend payment in conjunction with an already issued payment.

CHAPTER 6

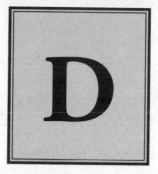

DEFINITIONS

Daily average revenue trades (DARTs): The measurement of the amount of trades a brokerage firm is able to handle on a daily basis. The measurement includes the cost of administrative and commission fees.

Dash to trash: Investors seek to invest in stocks and bonds that have lower purchase prices in order to get in the market. This happens during a bull market.

Days inventory: This calculation (inventory over day-to-day price on sales) reflects how well the company is performing on a daily basis. The least amount of inventory held over the days will project a great performance by the company. Adversely, higher inventory amounts equates to a weaker performance by the company.

Days payable: The amount of time a company has to repay obligations.

Days receivable: The amount of time a consumer has to pay for a product or service.

Days sales in accounts receivable: See *Days receivable*.

Days sales in inventory: See *Days inventory*.

Days sales outstanding: The amount of time a company will have before a payment can be considered income received.

Dead cat bounce: A fleeting upswing in a bear market that is followed by another dip.

Debasement: To decrease the amount an investment is worth.

Debenture bond: (1) The ability for a consumer to purchase a product or service without paying until a future date, or (2) a security given by a government agency to secure additional funds.

Debit balance: The amount reflects how much an individual, business, or corporation is obligated to pay to a third party; for example, money owed to a financial institution for a loan.

Debit memorandum: (1) A notification to an account holder from a financial institution about a charge against an account, like a service fee for insufficient funds. (2) During a sales transaction, the vendor may notify the other party about extra charges on the original purchase agreement.

Debit note: A statement for a customer to pay an amount in return for services to the company.

Debit: On the balance sheet, this represents a transaction recorded in the right column.

Debt extinguishment: In order to pay off an obligation, a creditor may accept a higher yield investment to relinquish the debt owed.

Debt for bond swap: To exchange the amount of debt for the price of an investment bond.

Debt service coverage: The amount of money required to pay off an obligation and a company's ability to pay it off.

Debt service: Money received to cover the payment of an obligation. Payments include interest.

Debt-to-capital ratio: Involves how much a company owes in obligations. If the ratio is high, the company holds more debt. Adversely, the company does not have that much debt if the ratio is low.

Debt-to-equity ratio: The measurement of how much a company has in equity to pay off obligations.

Debt-to-total-assets ratio: The measurement of how much income is pledged for paying off obligations. The calculation is expenses over income.

Debt/asset ratio: See *Debt-to-total-assets ratio.*

Debtor: When an individual, business, or corporation has to repay an obligation to another third party. Another third party can include financial institutions or government agencies.

Declaration date: (1) When a company will issue another dividend payment, or (2) the final time a stockholder has the right to place an option on the stock or bond.

Declining balance method: The allocation of a depreciation expense on the amount that is not depreciated.

Dedicated capital: The amount stock is listed based on par value. The most common type is treasury stock.

Deduction: Individuals or corporations are given the opportunity to subtract expenses from the total amount of income recognized. These expenses include childcare and health insurance.

Defensive acquisition: A company gains the ownership of another company during an aggressive move. Commonly, the move occurs during a time when the stock market is volatile.

Defensive interval: The amount of time a company is able to conduct business operations by not having to draw on other income sources. Other income sources can include real estate or investments.

Deferral type adjusting entry: A change in the general ledger accounts to reflect a cost that will be included in the next year.

Deferral: If a purchase has been paid for but has not been accounted for on the company's balance sheet. For example: insurance premium payments for the upcoming year.

Deferred acquisition costs (DAC): This involves holding off on recognizing costs related to insurance until the legal agreement has been signed by the insurance firm and the client.

Deferred charge: The application of a charge against an account. The charge will continue for the life of the asset.

Deferred credit: The amount of income recorded on a transaction, which has not been received.

Deferred debit: Amounts paid for before a transaction has occurred, like rent, contract fees, and interest payments.

Deferred expense: The initial transaction is recorded as income but will be later changed to an expense. For example, payment for office supplies at a fee of $50, but you only spend $25. The difference of $25 is recorded as an expense.

Deferred income tax: The difference of reported income tax in one year to income tax reported in previous years. An adjusting entry is made to make sure the account balances at the end of each accounting period.

Deferred revenue: Income that has been received for a product or service that has not been delivered.

Deferred tax asset: When a company utilizes an asset to reduce the amount of income taxes owed. This can only happen if there is a definite reason that a company will be able to afford operating costs for the next accounting period.

Deferred tax liability: Taxes a company must pay but not in the current accounting period. Taxes will be paid in a future year.

Deficit net worth: When the amount of expenses outweighs income coming in. For example, if the housing market tanks, a homeowner will owe more on the loan than what the property is currently valued at.

Deficit spending: How much a company exceeded over income reported.

Deficit: The result of overspending on expenses over total revenue received.

Defined benefit pension plan: How much an employer agrees to contribute to a retirement savings plan for employees.

Defined contribution pension plan: This agreement between employers and employees outlines how much will be contributed to employees and what type of retirement benefits will be received by the employees.

Delivery equipment: The category an accountant uses to identify equipment used to deliver goods and services for a company.

Delivery expense: The amount charged for freight fees. This involves freight received by the company and freight sent out by the company.

Demand deposits: When an account can be charged regardless of a notification to the account holder, like service fees.

Dematerialization: If a company recorded only paper transactions and then decides to utilize a more efficient method, like a computer tracking system. This often happens when a new business starts out with paper and then experiences tremendous growth in profits. The business will switch to an automated bookkeeping system.

Departmental overhead rate: The method of evaluating the costs associated with maintaining a department. The rate takes into account for direct and indirect costs as well as the amount of time it takes to manufacture a particular product.

Dependent variable: In order for a process to happen, another factor must be added to maintain the variability of the manufacturing operations. For example, one constant (dependent) is added to another constant (independent).

Depletion expense: The cost associated with taking off natural resource accounts at the end of an accounting period. The amount is also recorded as accumulated depreciation.

Depletion: How assets are deducted from operating expenses. This term mostly applies to companies that deal with energy and resources for production, like oil refineries.

Deposits in transit: Income that has been processed but not yet recorded by the bank.

Deposits: Transactions shown on bank statement that represent income received.

Depreciated cost: How much depreciation has been taken off the asset during the accounting period.

Depreciated — accelerated: Also referred to as *Accumulated depreciation.*

Depreciated — double declining balance: Utilizing the method of straight-line depreciation, this measurement of depreciation is doubled in the following years during the life of the asset.

Depreciation expense-equipment: Also referred to as *Accumulated depreciation-equipment.*

Depreciation expense: The amount taken for depreciation after the asset's useful life has ended.

Depreciation methods: There are several different types to calculate depreciation: straight-line, sum-of-the-year's digits, and double-declining.

Depreciation — sum-of-the-year's-digits: Also referred to as *Sum-of-the-years' method.*

Depreciation: If a company acquires a piece of equipment, the company allocates a cost for the usable life as long as the company retains ownership of the equipment. For example, buying a truck to transport goods to customers.

Depreciation — straight-line: Also referred to as *Straight-line method of depreciation.*

Dialing and smiling: A marketing technique for an investment broker who is trying to land new clients with a phone call and a bright, sunny attitude.

Digested security: When an investor has purchased an investment but has no intentions of doing anything to increase its value.

Digital option: An investment that retains a constant price payoff after the initial dividend payment has been made.

Dilutive acquisition: When an acquiring company takes over another company but does not receive an increase on the profit margin.

Direct access trading (DAT): An investor has quicker access to an investment brokerage firm through this online trading method.

Direct cost: To appropriate the correct price of an asset.

Direct costing: Also referred to as *Variable costing*.

Direct labor efficiency variance: This method is utilized to figure out how much time it took to produce a product over how many hours were allocated to finish the project.

Direct labor price variance: The cost of how many hours it takes to produce a product with a set amount of worked hours.

Direct labor quality variance: Also referred to as *Direct labor efficiency variance*.

Direct labor usage variance: Also referred to as *Direct labor price variance*.

Direct materials efficiency variance: Also referred to as *Standard direct materials cost*.

Direct materials inventory: A compilation of the components used to produce a product or service.

Direct materials price variance: See *Standard cost system*.

Direct materials quantity variance: Also referred to as *Standard direct materials cost.*

Direct materials usage variance: Also referred to as *Standard direct materials cost.*

Direct materials: The components to produce a product or service.

Direct method: The process of exchanging revenue from accrual to cash basis.

Direct profit: The total amount of sales for a company that does not include direct costs.

Direct write-off method: The ability to charge for an unpaid obligation because there is no possibility of collecting payment.

Disbursement: To give money in return for payment of a product or service.

Disclosure: To allow access to information regarding business transactions. For example, a corporation who will manufacture a new anti-cancer drug will have employees sign a disclosure agreement pertaining only to the information regarding the drug.

Discontinued operations: When a company stops business transactions. The portion that has been stopped must be accounted for on the company's financial statements.

Discount interest: A financial institution will take this amount upfront from the loan.

Discount on bonds payable: The amount used as a reduction on a bond that is considered to offset a debit and a credit entry. One account receives more, whereas the other account receives less.

Discount on notes payable: The amount used as a reduction on a note is considered to offset as a debit and a credit entry. One account receives less, whereas the other account receives more.

Discount on notes receivable: This is a transaction that reflects the amount taken from the principal of a note before the note becomes due. This involves a debit and a credit entry.

Discount rate: (1) The amount of interest to be calculated by financial institutions, or (2) how much an investment is valued on the current market.

Discounted cash flow model (DCF): The assessment of how well an investment will perform during the current market cycle. This rate is calculated by taking what the current amount of cash is valued over the current discount rate.

Discounted cash flow techniques: See *Discounted cash flow model*.

Discounted future benefits: Utilizing the discounted cash flow model, economists can project how much cash flow can be expected in subsequent years.

Discretionary expense: An account to record unusual purchases or fees for the course of business operations. For example, a meal at a 4-star restaurant for a prospective client.

Disinvestments: (1) To try to unload an investment during a financial crisis, or (2) a company will not put out more money on big expenses to retain a better profit margin for future investments.

Disposal of fixed assets: When a company wants to relinquish an asset, the company will sell the asset. The transaction will either have a positive or negative effect on the company's balance sheet.

The calculation is the price of the asset minus what the asset is currently valued at.

Distressed securities: Investments that have been affected by a company's insolvency issues. These investments are almost valued as worthless until the company's financial status has returned to normal or the company is sold to a solvent buyer.

Distributing syndicate: A combination of financial institutions in charge of managing investments traded on a public market.

Dividend declaration date: See *Declaration date.*

Dividend payout ratio: The amount an investor will receive in dividends over the life of the investment. The calculation is the amount of dividends over how much the total investment is worth.

Dividend yield: The determination of how much a company will pay in dividends according to how much the total investment is worth.

Dividend: The amount an investor acquires when owning shares of a company.

Dividends declared: When a company has issued a dividend payment, but the payment has not been sent to investors.

Dividends in arrears: This applies to preferred stockholders. The amount of dividends is given not on a time schedule but another determined date.

Dividends payable: When a company will issue dividend payments to stockholders.

Diworsification: Acquiring an investment that does not portray a good outcome for an investment plan and actually worsens the risk/return in the portfolio.

Doing the reverse desk: When an investment broker creates a hedge fund that projects the same yield return as other funds on the market.

Dollar — value LIFO method: This measurement uses the amount of inventory based on the price of inventory on hand. By using how much inventory was left to how much inventory was started with, the accountant can determine how much does the current amount inventory cost.

Dollar — value retail method: See *Dollar — value LIFO method.*

Dollar — weighted rate of return: The difference between the amount of cash and the amount of investments in the current market.

Donated surplus: When a company allocates investment funds to another company based on a shareholder's request. This transaction happens when an investor will try to generate a future stock purchase with the company.

Double budget: The method of not combining revenue and liabilities on the same balance sheet.

Double-dip recession: When the economy has a temporary bounce-back from a period of recession and there is another slip into a subsequent recession.

Double-entry accounting: The method of having two accounts for each transaction — one debit and one credit.

Double taxation: When a company issues dividends two times during the fiscal year. The dividends represent a tax on company revenue and revenue tax for shareholders receiving payments.

Double-declining balance depreciation method: Also referred to as *Depreciation — double declining balance.*

Double-entry bookkeeping: Also referred to as *Double-entry accounting.*

Downside: When the price of stock is affected by the dips in the market.

Draw: The amount of cash taken out of an account.

Drawing account: The area where a business owner takes out cash from the business. The implication: the amount of business income is decreased. The amount of cash taken out is not subjected to income taxes.

Dual-purpose fund: An investment that is created with two different types of stocks or bonds.

Due diligence: (1) The assurance that an investment transaction is valid, or (2) to act upon a situation with credibility.

Due on sale: This term applies when the full amount of a mortgage must be paid at the time of the sale or purchase of the property.

Dumbbell: Investments that have both components of short-term and long-term profit returns.

Duopoly: When two or more companies produce the same type of product or service in the same market sector.

CHAPTER 7

DEFINITIONS

Early exercise: To opt out of an investment or security before the maturity date is reached.

Earmarking: Money that is put toward the payment of a certain product or service.

Earned: The amount of income an individual, business, and corporation recognizes on a financial statement.

Earned premium: The total calculation of premium payments that were collected by the insurance company during a company's current accounting period.

Earnest money: When a consumer puts money down on a purchase with the intent to buy at a future date.

Earning asset: A valued instrument that produces revenue, like rent on a rental property owned by a company.

Earnings before interest and taxes (EBIT): The profit a company has before interest and tax payments are deducted from total net income.

Earnings before interest, taxes, depreciation, and amortization (EBITDA): The profit a company has before interest and tax payments, depreciation, and amortization is deducted from total net income.

Earnings before interest, taxes, depreciation, amortization, and rent (EBITDAR): The profit a company has before interest and tax payments, depreciation, amortization, and rent payments are deducted from total net income.

Earnings before taxes (EBT): The profit a company has before taxes are deducted from the total net income.

Earnings management: See *Cookie jar accounting*.

Earnings per share (EPS): The amount of income on shares held by investors.

Earnings quality: The validity of a company's reported income. An accountant reviews validation.

Earnings report: A document that highlights a company's financial status.

Earning the points: When the difference between a bid and the current value of the investment yields an increase on the profit return.

Earnings: The amount of revenue a business reports after expenses have been taken off the total net income.

Earnout: When a business owner tries to increase a revenue base during the sale of the business. This helps the business owner position himself or herself for a better financial structure during business negotiations.

Easement: The ability of an individual to operate or utilize a property even though the property is owned by another party. The problem with an easement occurs when the property is for sale and the ownership rights are in question.

Ease of movement: An evaluation method to determine how an asset's worth is related to the amount the asset is available for on the trading market.

Easy money: A term used by the Federal Reserve to determine how much cash must remain in the reserve to support the gross economic system.

Easy-to-borrow list: A compilation of investments that are readily attainable for buying and selling.

Eat your own dog food: A slang term used to describe a company utilizing in-house inventory to maintain corporate sustainability during a financial crisis.

Eating stock: Having to buy stock because there is a need to purchase but not a want to purchase. This happens when stockbrokers cannot find clients to purchase poorly performing stocks and must "eat" them.

EBIT margin: See *Earnings before taxes (EBT)*.

Economic blight: The bad affects of a destructive economic status on city hubs and main street towns. In recent times, investors have banded together to try to revitalize communities that have been hit hard by economic difficulties.

Economic entity assumption: Based on GAAP, an entity must be different from the financial interests of the company's owners.

Economic life: The valuation of an instrument based on the cost of the instrument during its useful life.

Economic lot size: The amount of inventory available for purchase at a lower cost.

Economic moat: This term was created by Warren Buffett to describe how companies overpower other companies that are in a similar line of business.

Economic order quantity model (EOQ): R. H. Wilson invented the Wilson model that appears to be closely matched to the EOQ model. This method evaluates a production cycle that used low inventory costs to speed up the production line.

Economic surplus: When there is a significant increase in assets over the amount of liabilities a company holds.

Economic think tank: A group of individuals who are responsible for formulating policies to support the work of the economy. Most of these groups receive financial help from private sources. This draws criticism about whether the financial support is derived from legal entities.

Economic value added (EVA): The method of evaluating a company's profit margin based on how much profit is recognized after other expenses and taxes are deducted.

Economic value: The measurement of how an asset is able to produce revenue.

Economy of scale: When a company wants to decrease the cost of manufacturing a product but still increase the company's profit margin, it will try to balance the budget by decreasing operation expenses.

Economy of scope: When a company tries to manufacture a different product but utilizes the same manufacturing equipment in order to increase the company's profit margin.

Effective debt: The total amount of obligations a company holds.

Effective interest rate method of amortization: The recognition of a bond expense based on the amount of interest amortized over the life of the bond.

Effective interest rate: Also referred to as *Effective rate*.

Effective net worth: The difference of a company's net income minus operating liabilities.

Effective rate: The method of calculating interest based on the current amortization schedule.

Efficiency ratio: The measurement of how well a company can manage income and expenses. The accounts monitored are accounts receivable and payable.

Efficiency variance: Also referred to as *Direct labor efficiency variance.*

Eighty/twenty rule: Developed by Italian-born Vilfredo Pareto, this formula referred to the fact that 20 percent of individuals in his country had 80 percent of the wealth. In present day, the broad definition is that in anything, a small number (20 percent) is vital and the rest (80 percent) are trivial. In business, it equates to 20 percent of a project necessitating 80 percent of an employee's time, energy, and resources.

Electronic funds transfer (EFT): The ability to send money, like employee payroll, from one account location to another through an online bank system.

Elephants: A catch phrase used to describe investment plans that incorporate a significant number of volume trades. One example of an elephant is an employee contribution pension plan.

Elevator pitch: A marketing strategy to hook the attention of potential clients in the time it takes for an elevator to travel from different floors. Investment brokers utilize this strategy to highlight new products offered by the investment firm.

Elliott wave theory: Developed by Ralph Nelson Elliott, this theory says that movements in the stock market gravitate like waves in the ocean. Like an ocean wave, the market moves in five steps up and three steps down.

Elm street economy: Unlike the big corners of Wall Street, the street corners of this street represent a small-town economic feel. The small-town mentality encompasses the economic structure in residential and town businesses.

Embedded option: An investment that is traded with the same investment type.

Embedded value (EV): To assess the value of life insurance policies, the method calculates the value of assets added to future revenue of the policy.

Embezzlement: When an individual steals funds from another individual through investments or other assets.

Emerging issues task force (EITF): Under the auspices of FASB, this association tackles issues dealing with future accounting practices.

Emolument: Payment for an individual who serves in a public office. This type of payment is legal as long as it is related to the individual's responsibilities associated with the public office.

Emotional neutrality: An investor must not let his or her emotions affect how he or she chooses to invest money in stocks or bonds. Investment brokers counsel clients to invest by thinking with their heads and not their hearts.

Employee fringe benefits: Compensation (other than wages) for employees. These benefits include health insurance and reimbursement for meals.

Employer payroll taxes: Taxes paid by employers on behalf of employees. For example, the Federal insurance contribution act (FICA) tax and Federal unemployment tax (FUTA).

Empty creditor: When a company decides to no longer do business with a company who can cover bad obligations.

End-of-the-month (EOM): This refers to looking into transactions that happened during the month and balancing the accounts when the month has ended.

End-of-the-year convention: This term came about after the infamous Enron debacle. It refers to using undesirable accounting methods (like cookie jar accounting) to project a favorable stock price for the company when the stock is at a low on the market.

Enduring purpose: A statement outlining a business or company's financial and business operations.

Entry point: The time when an investor decides to acquire an investment.

Equipment rental expense: If a company leases a piece of equipment, there must be a record on the balance sheet for a rent payment.

Equipment: Assets used by the company for manufacturing or operations, like delivery trucks.

Equity method: When a company holds stock options within another company, the company will evaluate how well the stock is performing.

Equity securities: A stock or bond a holder has within a company. The holder has rights to a definite amount of a company's revenue margin.

Equity value: See *Equity*.

Equity: The balance of income or loss once expenses are taken out for the accounting period.

Equivalent units of production: This calculation can be done by both the FIFO (First-in, first-out) method or a weighted average. The outcome will assess how many units are produced against how much it costs to produce one unit.

Escrow: (1) Cash or investments that must be handed over according to a written document between a lender and a customer, or (2) the place where a lender calculates how much a borrower has to pay on a loan.

Estimate: A projection of how much a product or service will cost or the amount of time it would take to manufacture a product.

Estimating inventory: Also referred to as *Cost of goods sold*.

Ex-dividend: A dividend has already been paid to a stockholder and no other subsequent payments will be made.

Examples: A windstorm causes damages to a manufacturing plant (considered a loss) or increased revenue due to a promotional sales technique (considered a gain).

Except-for-opinion: When an auditor cannot perform auditing duties on a company due to implications placed by the company or other management personnel.

Excess cash: When a company has more revenue on the balance sheet. If a company has more than 20 percent revenue, it is deemed an excess.

Exchange of dissimilar nonmonetary assets: The trade of a valued instrument for one that is not the same, like trading a piece of equipment for a parcel of land.

Exchange of similar nonmonetary assets: The trade of a valued instrument for one that is the same, like trading a cargo van for another cargo van.

Exemption: Another source to allow an individual or business owner to deduct amounts from gross income. A child can be used as an exemption on a tax return.

Expanded accounting equation: This method takes a closer look at an owner's equity in the company. The calculation is revenue minus liabilities minus what an owner has taken out of the company.

Expected value: This method is based on calculating a variable against a predicted number.

Expenditure: The ability to pay for an obligation or debt.

Expenses and losses: Both categories must be reported on a company's profit and loss statement.

Expenses: See *Expenditure.*

Expired: When a contract or agreement ends between one party and another.

Exploding the bill of materials: When materials are used in production, there are hierarchies for each component. Once each component is used, it is taken off the materials list.

Extinguishment of debt: Also referred to as *Debt extinguishment.*

Extraordinary item — gain/loss: Valued instruments that do not appear frequently on the company's balance sheet. These instruments can either be classified as a gain or loss.

Extraordinary repair: When a price of equipment needs maintenance that will ultimately enhance the performance of the production line. The transaction is reported as an expense. This does not involve an extraordinary item.

CHAPTER 8

DEFINITIONS

Factor: When a company relinquishes an asset from receivables to acquire another asset.

Factoring accounts receivable: If a company needs to acquire cash quickly to maintain business operations, the company may sell off accounts receivable. By doing this, the company can gain an influx of cash to sustain through a financial crisis.

Factoring: The recording of the relinquishment of an asset from receivables to the acquisition of another asset.

Factory burden: The overall cost in operating a manufacturing plant. The costs involved are labor, equipment expenses, and management costs.

Factory order: The cost of production invoices in a manufacturing plant.

Factory overhead: The costs associated in the manufacturing process, like a federal contract to produce a new research drug.

Fair market value (FMV): The current status of a real estate property in a dollar amount.

Fair rate of return: The amount a regulated agency is able to charge a customer for services. For example, a water treatment plant can charge for a fee for service.

False market: When skyrocketing prices dictate a strong pull in the market, investments with inflated premiums have been created. The exact value of an investment may be incorrect in this market.

Far option: An investment that does not have a set expiration time and is used with investments that carry larger premium payouts.

FAS: These are rules set by FASB for what are regulated accounting standards.

FASB 157: A ruling from FASB that keeps a control over companies who are involved in trading in public markets. Each company is broken down into different levels according to their trading status.

FASB interpretations: This is a compilation of all the FASB rulings.

FASB statements of accounting standards: Also referred to as *FASB statements of financial accounting concepts (SFAC).*

FASB statements of financial accounting concepts (SFAC): A statement prepared by FASB to highlight the history of proposed rulings for accounting practices.

FASB: Stands for the Financial Accounting Standards Board. Under the auspices of FASB, these regulations keep control over accounting practices for companies. FASB controls the Securities and Exchange Commission (SEC).

Fast market: A trading floor where heavy volume investments match up with riskier investments.

Fat cat: A slang term that associates bloated salaries and investments for chief executive officers (CEOs) and chief operating officers (COOs) of large companies.

Favorable variance: See *Standard cost system*.

Federal budget: The overall financial picture for the United States of America.

Federal income tax withholding payable: This involves an individual, business, or corporation to take exemptions from their federal tax base. Exemptions include dependents or health care expenses.

Federal insurance contributions act (FICA): This tax supports funding for Social Security and medicare.

Federal unemployment tax (FUTA): Employees put a portion of taxes towards funding programs for individuals who are unemployed or disabled.

Fee: When a company performs a service, income must be recorded on the balance sheet. The record happens when payment has been received.

Feeder fund: An investment plan created to be a pass through for a larger investment plan.

Fees earned: Payment made for services rendered by a consultant or an independent contractor. The consultant or contractor records this as revenue, whereas the company paying for the service records this as an expense.

Fence: A protective profit barrier set up for investments that take a hit on the trading market.

FICA expense-delivery: The company's record of payment of FICA taxes for the current accounting period that is for employees involved in the delivery sector of the company.

FICA expense-selling & admin: The company's record of payment of FICA taxes for the current accounting period that is for employees involved in the sales and administration sector of the company.

FICA expense — warehouse: The company's record of payment of FICA taxes for the current accounting period that is for employees involved in the warehouse sector of the company.

FICA tax payable: Also referred to as *Federal insurance contributions act (FICA)*.

Field of use: A clause enacted upon the use of a patent only for the purpose it was applied for.

FIFO cost flow assumption: Also referred to as *Cost flow assumption*.

FIFO method: This is based on allocating costs to merchandise that was put into inventory first.

Fighting the tape: Allowing an investment to be bought or sold on the trading market when the ticker reflects a down market. Many investors feel this practice should not happen, because it devalues the integrity of the investments.

Fill or kill (FOK): To place or destroy an investment transaction.

Finality of payment: Once money has been received or deposited into a vendor's account, the transaction is considered final.

Financial Accounting Foundation: This organization is responsible for the managerial duties of FASB. This organization handles member relations, financial reporting for FASB, and oversees the AICPA.

Financial accounting: The act of overseeing the financial operations of companies based on accounting standards.

Financial asset: A valued instrument bound by a contractual obligation. An example of an asset is a bond.

Financial capital: Money needed for initial start-up costs to run a business.

Financial condition: The current financial picture of a company. This takes into consideration the amount of revenue on hand versus how many expenses are on the books.

Financial distress: An individual, business, or company's inability to generate revenue when there are too many debts.

Financial health: Also referred to as *Financial condition*.

Financial leverage: The measurement of how a company handles the management of paying obligations.

Financial ratios: Tools for an accountant to evaluate the performance of a company. One type of ratio widely used is the price-earnings ratio.

Financial reporting: The measurement of how well a company is performing.

Financial statement analysis: To evaluate the financial status of a company. An accountant will perform several duties, like profit and loss analysis, oversee management practices, and prepare financial statements.

Financial statement: A document detailing the financial aspects of a company.

Financial structure: Listed on the balance sheet, an accountant will analyze categories involving revenue-producing activities such as acquisition of equipment and cash deposits.

Financing activities: When a company acquires securities and investments to generate more revenue.

Finished goods inventory (FGI): Inventory on hand that has not been sold. Until a sale is made, a company will carry the inventory as an asset.

Fire sale: When stocks and bonds are valued at a low price on the market. Investors are encouraged to invest but warned to proceed with caution because of the low price.

First in, still here (FISH): When a company is not able to sell inventory that was either purchased or produced first.

Fiscal year: Unlike a calendar year, this term covers the actual accounting period for a company.

Fixed accounting: This method is used by non-profit and government agencies. Each category is called a "fund" and revenue and expenses are allocated to a particular fund.

Fixed asset: A valued instrument that has a longer useful life, like land.

Fixed budget: A document prepared based on actual costs according to a current production schedule.

Fixed cost: A price set without any changes made.

Fixed expenses: Also referred to as *Fixed cost.*

Fixed income: Profit from investments that produce interest.

Fixed manufacturing overhead applied: Also referred to as *Standard cost variances.*

Fixed manufacturing overhead budget variance: See *Standard cost variances.*

Fixed manufacturing overhead incurred: Prices that will be evident during the manufacturing process but will never change, like depreciation on a piece of manufacturing equipment.

Fixed manufacturing overhead volume variance: This term is also referred to as *Standard cost variance.*

Fixed overhead budget variance: This term is also referred to as *Standard cost variance.*

Fixed overhead spending variance: This term is also referred to as *Standard cost variance.*

Fixed rate loan: The amount of interest does not change on this type of obligation; an individual does not have to be concerned with changes in interest rates.

Fixed-change coverage ratio: A measurement of how well a company can cover operating costs. The calculation is interest and taxes over the price plus interest accrued.

Flexible budget: A document that represents revenue and expenses that can change due to variations in business operations. For example, the budget may have $50 for office supplies but instead only $25 was expensed. The budget can be changed to reflect the $25 difference.

Float: (1) Checks that have been issued but not have been paid, or (2) acquiring new investments through another investment firm.

Floor: The cost of an investment at the bottom of the trading market.

Flow through equity (FTE): The amount of profit that will be delegated to stockholders by another company other than the issuing company, like a limited liability corporation.

Foam the runway: In a valiant effort to save a company from claiming bankruptcy, like airports deluge a runway with foam to prevent a horrific crash, company personnel seek a way to raise funds to resuscitate the company's bottom line.

FOB destination: When freight is received by a customer, the customer handles the responsibility of all shipping charges.

FOB shipping point: Freight charges are paid by the customer before the customer receives products or services.

Focus report: A document that reflects the performance of investments on a trading market. This document allows investors to see how much profit or loss was calculated during the month.

Foot: To total the balances in each column on a worksheet.

Footnotes: Serve as further documentation to explain accounting practices on a company's financial statements.

Forensic accounting: This method of accounting deals with financial procedures that have been challenged or charged as illegal. One example of forensic accounting is examining insurance fraud claims.

Form 10-K: If a company is publicly traded, the SEC will issue a document highlighting a company's performance record for potential and current investors.

Form 10-Q: Unlike the Form 10-K, this document highlights a company's performance every 4 months instead of monthly.

Forward-looking statement: A document based on projecting future sales and expenses based on current financial figures. This document is used by managers as a projection too but does not reflect what current financial figures are.

Franchise: A special license to produce or sell products or services that is controlled by the state and local laws where the license has been incorporated.

Fraption: An investment strategy used to secure a lower interest rate for a certain time in order to absorb a higher premium cost.

Free cash flow (FCF): The ability for a company to handle operating expenses after cash disbursements have been made.

Free cash flow for the firm (FCFF): The ability for a company to handle operating expenses after cash disbursements and investment payments have been made.

Free cash flow per share: How well a company is performing based on how much revenue is generated from the number of investments held by investors.

Free cash flow to equity (FCFE): The amount of money left for stockholders after the company pays for operating expenses.

Free cash flow yield: See *Free cash flow (FCF)*.

Free on board (FOB): The customer does not have to pay shipping charges but is responsible for the products or services once it reaches the customer. Once the product reaches the destination, the supplier is no longer liable for damages.

Freight analysis framework (FAF): This method projects how much freight is transported yearly throughout transportation highways and roadways.

Freight-in: See *Delivery expense.*

Freight-out: See *Delivery expense.*

Fringe benefits: See *Employee fringe benefits.*

Front fee: The payment required to initiate a purchase agreement.

Front office: A method utilized in the hospitality industry that calculates room rates, efficiency standards, and credit card purchases.

Full disclosure principle: Like a footnote, this method outlines documentation regarding accounting practices used by a company.

Fully depreciated: When a valued instrument has met the level of depreciation costs in relations to the instrument's useful life.

Functional classification expense: A method to categorize fixed expenses.

Functional currency: The availability of money to operate a business.

Fund accounting: This type of accounting is used by non-profit organizations. This method focuses on how the organizations meet their business objectives without a huge concern over garnishing a great profit return.

Fund balance: How much an account is valued at after expenses are taken from revenue.

Fungibles: An investment that can be used to secure another investment.

Furlough: A solution to avoid mass employee termination by reducing the amount of days employees work or closing business operations on certain days.

Furniture and fixtures: The category used by an accountant to classify permanent items used in business operations, like computer desks and monitors.

Furthest out: This term applies to investment contracts that will mature before the end of the current month.

Futures: An agreement between a client and a vendor for the purchase of stocks or other securities like a mutual fund.

Future value (FV): The amount an investment of a valued instrument is rated for a date not specified. The calculation is interest times how many years the investment is held for.

Future value of an annuity due: Like calculating future value, this method utilizes a specific number of times payments would be made plus interest accrued.

Future value of an ordinary annuity: See *Future value of an annuity due.*

CHAPTER 9

DEFINITIONS

Gadfly: A creative term to describe when an investor chooses to attend shareholder meetings with the intention to cause problems there.

Gain contingency: When a company is involved in a lawsuit that seem like it will go in its favor, the company will record an increase on the balance sheet.

Gain on retirement of bonds: When a company will make a move to recapture expired bonds, the company can record an increase on the balance sheet. The calculation is current value minus the price of the bond at the time of recall. For example, current value is $1,000 − $500 (price of bond) = $500 increase.

Gain on sale of assets: A company will record an increase on the balance sheet when there is a sale transaction for a valued instrument. For example, the sale of a piece of furniture used in an office.

Gain on sale of automobile: This transaction is recorded from the difference between what the vehicle sold for and how much the vehicle is currently valued at. For example, a car is valued at

$2,500 but sold for $3,000. The difference of $500 is recorded as an increase on the balance sheet.

Gain on sale of equipment: This transaction is recorded when a company sells off equipment that was used in business operations.

Gain on sale of investments: The amount of profit recognized after a company elects to sell investments. This is recorded as an increase on a balance sheet.

Gain on sale of land: A company increases the amount in the land category when a sale has been recorded.

Gain or loss on sale of long-term asset: A company will record either an increase or decrease when the sale of a valued instrument has been recorded.

Gains: The increase in the amount of profit as a result of sales of valued instruments. The amount is recorded on a company's financial statement.

Gap ratio: The measurement of a company's short-term investments against short-term expenses to see how much profit is recognized when the investments become due.

Garnishment payable: A company must record wages for an employee who is involved in a legal action even though the employee did not receive wages earned.

Garnishment: During a legal action, a company will not relinquish payroll to an employee involved in the case. Once the ruling has been made, the company has to obey according to the outcome of the proceedings.

Gatekeeper: When an individual wishes to engage in an extended investment plan, the individual must adhere to certain rules before the plan is carried out.

Gathering in the stops: When investment brokers will initiate a stop order to force the prices of stocks lower so investors will buy at the lower price.

GDP per capita: An estimate of how much an individual spends as a consumer compared to the total population spending on products and services.

Gearing: See *Financial leverage*.

General and administrative overhead: The amount it takes to run daily operations of a business.

General fund: Used in businesses and agencies that are open to the public, this account holds the revenue and expense balances like a public school system.

General journal entry: The transaction is recorded as a debit or credit in the general journal.

General journal: The place where transactions are recorded as revenue and expenses.

General ledger account: A category for revenue and expenses in the balance sheet and income statement.

General ledger: This area keeps balances in both the balance and income statement.

Generally Accepted Accounting Principles (GAAP): The regulations developed to manage accounting methods for companies. These rules are enforced to keep a watchful eye over accounting practices, profit and loss, investments, and management.

Generational accounting: A type of accounting that monitors the current economic status based on previous years to determine how the economy will function in the next generation gap.

Generic securities: Investments created by the issuance of financial notes or loans. These investments last only one year.

Gentlemen's agreement: An informal deal for work to happen between a vendor and consumer. This agreement becomes a problem when either party decides he or she no longer wants to be involved with carrying out the agreement.

Ghosting: Considered to be an inappropriate action, this happens when two or more companies try to influence the reduction of stock prices and ultimately challenge the value of the stock.

Giffen good: When a consumer tries to buy a popular item that is overpriced when the demand is higher for the item.

Gifted stock: An investment passed from one individual to another to reduce the amount of taxes each individual has to pay.

Gilt-edged bond: An investment tied to a company that has been rated as a fiscally and responsible stable entity.

Ginzy trade: Deemed inappropriate behavior, this type of trade allows a high volume of stocks or bonds to be bought or sold for less than the security's current value.

Give up: When an investment broker will put a transaction through for another investment broker but will take full credit for the investment when the transaction is recorded. The question arises: Who is entitled to the commission fee on this transaction? This method is highly scrutinized, and many investment firms try to avoid this practice.

Global investment performance standards (GIPS): Regulations developed for firms that deal with investments on publicly traded markets. These regulations ensure that the reporting on investments is accurate for investors.

Godfather offer: An agreement to take over assets from one company during a potential hostile buyout. Coining the phrase from *The Godfather,* the acquiring company gives the desired company an offer it cannot refuse.

Going concern assumption: An assessment made on how a company is performing and can the company withstand changes in the economy.

Golden parachute: A safety net, like a salary and benefit package, to help management personnel from an acquired company during a change in company leadership.

Good output: The result of a good functioning production system. A company measures product performance based on the quality of products and services it has been manufacturing.

Goodwill: The cost given that measures the quality and efficiency of a business owner's reputation.

Go shop period: The ability of a company to entertain other investment offers even though the company has entered into a purchase contract with another party.

Graveyard market: The last sequence in the bear market. Depending on their investment style, investors have either done well or poorly in this type of market.

Greenshoe option: The ability of a stockbroker to offer more stocks to clients even though the original stock issue had a specific amount of shares to be sold.

Greenwashing: When a corporation supports the efforts of going green but, in turn, damages the ecosystem by manufacturing harmful products or providing detrimental services.

Gridlock: When a company cannot perform daily business operations due to an upcoming, unmanageable financial crisis.

Grinder: A creative name for an individual who invests in the stock market frequently but does not experience a high return on profit.

Gross block: The amount of valued instruments a company has. The amount does not include depreciable costs on long-term assets.

Gross income: The amount of revenue recognized before expenses are taken out.

Gross expense ratio: Also referred to as *Before reimbursement expense ratio.*

Gross margin: Also referred to as *Gross profit.*

Gross pay: The amount of wages earned by an employee before the appropriate taxes are taken out.

Gross profit margin: Also referred to as *Net profit margin.*

Gross profit method of estimating inventory: Also referred to as *Cost of goods sold.*

Gross profit percentage: Also referred to as *Net profit margin.*

Gross profit ratio: Also referred to as *Net profit margin.*

Gross profit: The amount of revenue recognized after the sales of products and services has been taken out.

Gross revenue: Also referred to as *Net profit margin.*

Growth rate: Also referred to as *Compound annual growth rate (CAGR).*

Gunslinger: A slang term for an investment broker who is always searching for the next big investment profit payoff.

Gut spread: An investment that is acquired to yield a high rate of profit in a short amount of time before stock is devalued on the market.

Gypsy swap: Repurposing stock from one individual to another to increase the dividend payout for both individuals.

CHAPTER 10

DEFINITIONS

Haircut: (1) The proportion of a cost that is different from the current value of a stock or bond, or (2) a fraction of an asset's cost that is applied to profit return.

Half commission man: An individual who tries to engage new clients to buy investments through a particular investment firm. The individual will receive one half of the fee earned, and the other half is retained by the investment firm.

Half stock: An investment that holds a $50 par value.

Halo effect: When a consumer does comparative research on two similar products and tries to make a decision on which is the best product to purchase for the quality and price listed.

Hamada equation: A method used to determine how well a company handles the payment of liabilities.

Hammer: When an investment is affected by a decrease in the stock market before the stock reaches a bottom price.

Handle: The full cost of an investment purchase.

Hands-off investor: An individual who participates in stock options of a company but chooses to remain behind the scenes.

Hands-on investor: An individual who participates in stock options of a company and wants to be a part of every decision made regarding stockholders.

Hard call protection: The portion of a bond that a company is unable to redeem.

Hard skills: Tactical strategies that are taught to individuals who want to have careers in financial and investment accounting, because it takes a thick skin to handle the ups and downs of a demanding profession.

Hard-to-borrow list: A compilation of stocks and bonds that are not easily attainable for buying or selling.

Headline inflation: A rough estimate that is reported every month based on the Consumer Price Index.

Health insurance expenses for delivery, selling, administration, and warehouse: The company's record of health insurance costs paid during the accounting period that involves employees working the delivery, sales, administration, and warehouse departments.

Health Insurance Portability and Accountability Act (HIPAA): Provides protection for patients from medical personnel decisions to disclose medical and financial information to third parties. This act was designed to regulate patient identity theft and insurance fraud.

Health reimbursement account: An account set up by employers to reimburse employees for medical expenses that were paid out of pocket.

Health Savings Act: A plan developed for individuals who need additional coverage for medical expenses that are not covered by traditional health insurance plans.

Hedge: An investment strategy used to counterbalance the effect of price changes on a valued instrument.

Hedge accounting: A type of accounting that involves the treatment of a hedge fund the same as accounting for other investments. The basis behind this accounting method is to utilize only one market value for all investments.

Hedge fund: A compilation of various high-risk investments designed to yield a high-profit return.

Hedge fund manager: An individual who is responsible for the management and operations of a hedge fund.

HedgeStreet®: A computer-driven trading market that allows investors to trade or purchase hedge funds based on activities reported across the Web.

Held order: An option that has been transferred quickly to a stock transaction.

Held-to-maturity securities: Investments a company will hold on to until the investments reach the retirement date.

Hell or high water contract: An agreement that outlines payment for goods or services whether or not the consumer has the funds to pay for it.

Help-wanted index (HWI): This list identifies the areas in which businesses and companies are seeking individuals for employment opportunities.

Herd instinct: When a group of investors feel vulnerable about stock prices and make a decision to sell based on a group-minded mentality.

Hiccup: A brief halt in individual or company business operations due to a shift in economic status or a legal issue.

Hidden asset: A valued instrument held by a company but not reported on a balance sheet.

Hidden values: An instrument that a company holds but does not appear on a balance sheet, like a patent for a new machine.

High-flyer: A stock that has enjoyed the benefits of being on the top of the leader board in profit margin and volume sales.

High-low method: An estimate of how much cost it will be to produce a product based on the company's highest cost price and lowest cost price during the accounting period.

High minus low (HML): This method evaluates the short- and long-term profit margins for a stock or bond to determine how well the stock or bond will perform in the future.

Historical cost: The value of an asset based on the price it was when a product was first produced.

Historical exchange rate: The comparison of money tables from prior to current years. This method calculates the changes in the rates to project how the market will do in future years.

Hockey stick bidding: When an investment broker offers a slice of an investment for purchase at an inflated price. In some investment firms, this practice is deemed unfair, and it opens firms up to being charged for fraud.

Holding gain/loss: A company may recognize either revenue or expenses in relation to the changes in prices based on assets in the current inventory. The record of an increase or decrease is reported as a footnote on the financial statement.

Holding period return/yield: The amount of profit or loss recognized on a company's investments. The calculation is the amount of income over how much the investment was worth at the start.

Holiday, vacation, sick days expense for delivery, sales, administration, and warehouse: The amount of personal time given to employees for employees who work in the delivery, sales, administration, and warehouse departments.

Honcho: A creative phrase that refers to the ringleader in a company or organization.

Honorarium: Compensation given to an individual for a service provided. This individual is not employed by the group providing the compensation. One example of an honorarium is compensation for a symposium at a writer's conference.

Horizontal analysis: The method of evaluating the rate of profit on an investment by projecting increases over several years. For example, if a company received a 15 percent profit increase in the previous quarter, an accountant will project another 15 percent profit increase for the next quarter.

Hostile bid: An offer to purchase a vulnerable company from a financially secure company.

House call: When an investment firm contacts an investor about the financial status of his or her investment portfolio. This happens when an investor's account is being depleted because of the changes in the investment marketplace.

House poor: When an individual spends well above his or her means and cannot afford basic necessities.

Hurdle rate: The amount of money it takes for a new investor to realize a profit on his or her investment.

Hybrid fund: Also referred to as *Blend fund*.

CHAPTER 11

DEFINITIONS

Identifiable intangible asset: A valued instrument that a company holds for a greater profit return. For example, a new marketing technique for a sales promotion. Although this is something you cannot see, it adds value to the company.

Idle funds: An account that has money in it but has remained inactive.

Illusory profits: See *Phantom profits*.

Impairment charge: The ability to relinquish products or services that are considered to be damaged or unusable.

Impairment of long-lived assets: In order for a company to relinquish assets that it considers to be damaged or unusable, the company must make sure it is a reasonable charge as to why the asset is no longer viable.

Impairment: A loss in revenue due to economical changes.

Implicit interest rate: Refers to a loan that has not identified an interest rate. For example, a person will pay $50 per month for 6 months instead of paying $285 in cash. The interest rate was not agreed upon but the customer will pay $15 extra in interest.

Imprest amount: See *Petty cash*.

Imputed interest: Although payment has not been made, interest will be calculated for payment.

Imputed value: A valued instrument will be listed on a company's financial statement based on historical cost and not at the current value of the asset.

In specie: From the Latin term meaning "in actual form," this is an asset that will be recorded as it appears and will not be converted for liquidation if a financial crisis arises.

In the black: A slang phrase referring to a company that will have enough revenue to cover operating expenses.

In the red: A slang phrase referring to a company that is burdened by operating expenses and is unable to generate revenue.

Inactive asset: A valued instrument not being used in current business operations. For example, a plow only used when another one needs to be repaired.

Income from operations: See *Operating income*.

Income statement: See *Profit and loss statement*.

Income summary statement: See *Temporary account*.

Income tax depreciation: Under the guidelines of the Internal Revenue Service, depreciation expenses are an allowable deduction from the gross income tax base.

Income tax expenses: Certain activities are allowed to be deducted from the gross income tax base, like dependent care, office supplies for a self-employed writer, and upgrading a roof with solar panels.

Income taxes payable: A line item on a company's financial statement to reflect how much taxes the company paid for the accounting period.

Income: Revenue recognized after operating expenses have been deducted.

Incoming averaging: To calculate income taxes based on prior year amounts. This method is no longer valid because of the revised tax laws in 1986.

Incremental analysis: The method of evaluating projects based on the differences of income and expenses. This determines which project will produce a larger profit.

Incremental cost: The price to manufacture one product.

Incremental internal rate of return: This combines two areas — incremental cost and cash flow. If the price of the product is $5 and then cash flow predicted is $10, the company will want to project a sales figure of $15 per item.

Incremental revenue: The amount of profit associated with how many products where manufactured for one production unit. If the product costs $2 to produce and 50 products were completed, then $100 will be considered a profit.

Incurred: A charge for a product or service received or delivered.

Indenture: A document binding two separate parties in a financial transaction, like a bond sale agreement.

Independent auditor: An individual who performs auditing functions for a company but is not an employee of the company.

Independent contractors: Non-salaried employees who perform regular duties assigned by the company.

Independent variable: Used in cost accounting practices, this is a constant that can only be changed by a set of other constants.

Index amortizing note (IAN): A security that has a payoff rate linked to the current market interest rate.

Indirect cost: An expense that is used in business operations but does not affect the manufacturing of a product or service, like office supplies.

Indirect labor costs: The amount allocated for labor hours or activities that are not related to the manufacturing process, like the lighting surrounding a finishing machine.

Indirect labor: The usage of time by employees who are not related to the manufacturing process, like the salary of a CEO.

Indirect manufacturing costs: An expense related to the manufacturing process but not directly associated with the product or service like depreciation of plant equipment.

Indirect materials: Items used that are not directly associated with manufacturing, like polish for the handles of a motor crank.

Indirect method: The process of exchanging revenue into a cash-based accounting system.

Individual development account (IDA): A starter fund for people who need extra help saving for certain purposes, such as college tuition and business expenses.

Inflation accounting: An accountant will correct financial statements that were prepared with historical costs and not actual costs.

Insolvent: When an individual, business, or corporation is unable to cover expenses due to lack of supporting income.

Institute of Management Accountants (IMA): An organization that oversees the management training and regulations for individuals who are certified management accountants.

Institutional Brokers' Estimate System (IBES): A database that was established by the Lynch, Jones, and Ryan brokerage. It is used to compile various analyst forecasts on future earnings for many publicly traded companies in the United States and helps investors make decisions regarding potential investments.

Insurance expense: The amount that is recorded for payment of insurance during an accounting period. This expense can also be accounted for in future years if the payment remains the same.

Insurance: Protection for an individual, business, or corporation in the event of liabilities or damages.

Intangible assets: A valued instrument used in a company's business operations. An example of an intangible asset is a research development contract.

Intangible cost: The amount allocated to an action that does not apply to a tangible asset, like the cost for advertising in a magazine.

Interest cover: When a company is able to afford interest payments after revenue has been calculated.

Interest earned: See *Times interest earned (TIE)*.

Interest expense: The amount allocated as interest payments made by a company.

Interest income: The amount allocated as interest received by company investments.

Interest payable: The record of how much interest has been paid on investments.

Interest receivable: A company will record the profit recognized on interest payments from investments.

Interest revenues: The record of interest payments at the point where the money has been received. The payments are reported on the balance sheet.

Interim financial statement: A document highlighting a company's financial status throughout the year instead of quarterly.

Internal audit: An individual who performs an audit on a company's accounting system. An auditor can be an independent or an employee of the company.

Internal expansion: When a company is able to increase business operations without outside activities (advertising and marketing).

Internal financing: A company can create new products or services without the help of outside funding (banks or investors).

Internal growth rate: See *Internal financing*.

Internal rate of return (IRR): See *Economic rate of return*.

Internal Revenue Service (IRS): This organization is responsible for the tax regulations concerning individuals, businesses, and corporations in the United States.

Interperiod tax allocation: When an income tax discrepancy conflicts with an accounting system following GAAP, an adjustment must be made to reflect a change in policy. For example, the IRS determines an asset's worth based on the time limit of 7 years, whereas the GAAP determines an asset's worth as long as it is being used. An accountant will make the change in a footnote to the difference in policy.

Interpolated Yield Curve (I Curve): A yield curve derived using on-the-run treasuries.

Interpretations: See *Accounting Principles Board (APB)*.

Interval measure: The measurement of how a company will be able to operate with a current amount of money available.

Intraperiod tax allocations: See *Interperiod tax allocation*.

Introducing broker (IB): An investment specialist who brings new clients to the firm but does not handle investment transactions for the client.

Inventoriable cost: The amount of inventory in stock.

Inventory carrying costs: See *Carrying cost of inventory*.

Inventory conformity rule: If a company elects to use a LIFO or FIFO method for inventory purposes, the company cannot change the method during an accounting period. These methods are used for calculations and preparation of a company's financial statements. If the methods are changed, implications of fraud could occur.

Inventory shrinkage: See *Shrinkage*.

Inventory turnover ratio: To determine how much inventory has been either put up for sale or changed due to damages. The calculation is the amount of sales over how much has been held in stock.

Inventory: Products or services a company has until a sales transaction has been made.

Investing activities: See *Cash flow from investing activities*.

Investing: The decision to pledge money into investments and securities in order to increase personal or business income.

Investment flows: See *Cash flow from investing activities.*

Investment in another company: When a company decides to purchase a security from a third party.

Investment revenues: The amount of profit recognized from investments.

Investment securities: The area where a financial institution records information about stockholder's accounts.

Invoice: A document that represents an agreement of the purchase of goods or services from a company to a consumer. This document includes the terms of payment for the goods or services.

CHAPTER 12

DEFINITIONS

Job order cost sheet: The document that represents the costs it requires to perform a particular job.

Job order system: The method of allocating costs to each job listed for production.

Joint cost: When two different products share the same price it takes to manufacture one product.

Joint product: When a product is taken off one production line and finished on another; it takes two machines to produce the same product.

Journal entry: The record of a transaction that occurs when it happens. The entry must have a corresponding increase and decrease to balance the account.

Journal: Area where transactions are accounted for. This includes a ledger or financial statement.

Journalize: To add transactions to the journal.

Junior capital pool (JCP): A company that issues stock options in lieu of being an operational business structure. This practice is only regulated in Canada.

Junk bonds: This type of investment yields a great return but offers no risk protection if the bond fails.

Just-in-time (JIT): During the manufacturing process, materials must be used within that moment for the process to produce a quality product. If not, the company will be stuck with unusable inventory.

CHAPTER 13

DEFINITIONS

Keogh plan: A type of plan set up for retirement benefits for business owners who need to pay for out-of-pocket expenses.

Kickback: Giving money to an individual to influence a decision in favor of the person who has offered payment.

Kicking the tires: A creative term to describe how a potential investor shops around for an investment brokerage firm.

Kids in parents' pockets eroding retirement savings (KIPPERS): When an adult child moves back home because he or she is unable to afford the expenses of living on his or her own, many parents often have to dip into their retirement accounts to absorb the extra expenses.

Kill: To destroy an investment transaction before it has been recorded in the system.

Killer bees: The saving grace for a company that was in the process of being taken over during a hostile bidding war.

Kiting: The process of using another bank to cash checks when a current checking or money market account is unable to support the transaction. Because of possible fraudulent activity, many banks do not allow this to happen.

CHAPTER 14

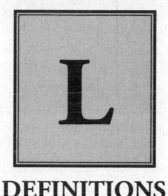

DEFINITIONS

Labor burden: When a company has trouble paying off indirect operating expenses, like lighting for a building.

Labor rate variances: See *Direct labor rate variance.*

Labor variances: Same as *Direct labor rate variance* or *Direct labor efficiency variance.*

Land improvements: Upgrades to increase the value of a property.

Land: An asset that is used for personal or business use.

Lead time: The time difference between when a product is produced to when a product has been sold.

Learning curve: In assessing labor costs, an accountant will factor in how to decrease the amount of labor time without decreasing the amount of production hours or quality.

Lease: See *Capital lease.*

Leaseback: When a company will give an opportunity to reuse a property to an individual or business that previously rented the property.

Leasehold improvements: On a rental space, either party is able to make upgrades on the property. Upgrades are considered to be part of depreciation charges, but it extends the usable nature of the property.

Ledger cash: The amount of money listed in the revenue accounts of a company's financial statements.

Ledger: A list of all company accounts, including balance sheet, journal, and accounts payable.

Legal capital: The current values listed for common stock on a company's financial statement.

Legal defeasance: If outstanding debts occurred on a bond, the lender has the ability to make sure the debts are paid before the lender considers the bond paid in full.

Lessee: An individual, business, or corporation that pays money for a property or instrument that they do not own.

Lessor: An individual, business, or corporation that offers products and services to customers who do not own them.

Letter of credit: A statement made by a lender stating a borrower is in good faith standing of being able to repay an amount agreed upon for goods or services.

Leverage company: See *Financial leverage.*

Leverage: See *Financial leverage.*

Liability: Costs created by the operation of the business that are considered expenses, like employee wages.

Lien: Staking ownership on another person's personal property.

LIFO conformity rule: See *Inventory conformity rule.*

LIFO method: This is based on allocating costs to merchandise that was put into inventory last.

LIFO reserve: The amount of inventory used in the LIFO method compared to the amount of inventory used in the FIFO method.

Like-for-like sales: The method of comparing current year sales figures to prior years sales figures to determine what type of products moved quicker than others.

Limited liability company (LLC): A structure formed to operate business functions but does not have the legal support like a corporation. An LLC is governed under different business rules than a regular business or corporation, but it still must follow GAAP.

Line of credit: A relationship between a lender and a client to compensate for extra expenses incurred by the client during the life of the loan.

Liquidating dividend: If a company is claiming bankruptcy or will cease business operations, the company will issue this type of payment to shareholders. Payments are based on how many shares a shareholder has in the company.

Liquidation of LIFO layers: A company will relinquish inventory that has been deemed unusable with the LIFO method. By doing this, the company is able to reduce costs and achieve a lower tax rate.

Liquidation value: How much a company is worth after the company sells off assets that were converted to cash.

Liquidity ratios: The method of figuring out how to convert assets to cash, like the current ratio.

Liquidity: The ability of a company to sell off assets quickly in a financial crisis.

Loan amortization schedule: A statement that outlines how much will be amortized for the life of an asset.

Loans receivable: A record of how much money needs to be paid on loans outstanding.

Lock-box system: An area where important documents are stored safely in the event the business property is destroyed or theft is attempted.

Long-term assets: Instruments that will not expire at the end of the accounting period and will be transferred to the next year's accounting period, like equipment.

Long-term investments: Securities that will not mature during the accounting period but will be transferred to the next year's accounting period, like a stock certificate.

Long-term liabilities: Debts owed by a company that are carried on to the next year's balance sheet.

Lookback option: A provision that allows investors to utilize previous profit return history to determine how much profit can be recognized in the long term for the option.

Loophole: A way for an individual to legally terminate a contract with another party because of a misunderstanding or mistake in the language of the contract.

Losing the points: When the difference between a bid and the current value of the investment yields a decrease on the profit return.

Losing your shirt: When an investor is caught up in a bad investment strategy and he or she is moving toward having to bear a huge loss that could cause him or her to lose everything — including his or her shirt.

Loss carryback: The IRS will allow a company that has suffered a loss in the current year to apply the loss to a previous tax return in order to reduce the heavy burden of tax liabilities and implications. This option must be recorded on the balance sheet for the next accounting period.

Loss carryforward: The IRS will allow a company that has suffered loss in the current year to apply the loss to next year's tax return in order to reduce the heavy burden of tax liabilities and implications. This option must be recorded on the balance sheet for the next accounting period.

Loss contingency: See *Gain contingency.*

Loss disallowance rule (LDR): When the IRS stops a corporation from filing one tax return to cover the corporation and other pieces of the corporation that are owned by a third party. This prevents a company from trying to release any losses incurred by the separate entity.

Loss from labor strike: The financial impact of a labor strike can be accounted for on a company's financial statement as a loss of income.

Loss from lawsuit: The financial impact of litigation proceedings can be accounted for on a company's financial statement as loss of income.

Loss given default (LGD): The amount of funds that are no longer recoverable after a consumer cannot make loan payments.

Loss on sale of assets: A company will record a decrease in income on the balance sheet when the company has to sell off assets in liquidation.

Loss on sale of computer, equipment, land, and truck: A company will record a decrease in income on the balance sheet because of selling computers, equipment, land, and trucks that are valued lower than what their actual purchase price was.

Loss: When operating expenses outweigh generated income.

Low-balance method: To figure out the amount of interest by using the smallest total that has been in the account.

Lower of cost or market (LCM): Based on the idea of conservatism, companies should try to use a lower price for inventory costs.

CHAPTER 15

DEFINITIONS

Major repairs: See *Extraordinary repairs.*

Make or buy decision: When a company is trying to figure out what is the better use of costs — either manufacture the product to sell or purchase the product and sell.

Managed earnings: An illegal practice in which a company will project a higher profit margin to attract investors.

Management's discussion and analysis: This statement provided by a company's management department highlights the financial operations for investors. This statement is included in the Form 10-K.

Managerial accounting: This method of accounting focuses on the management practices of a company. The issues dealing with this type of accounting are manufacturing, costing methods, and budgeting for production.

Manufacturing cell: The outlay of a production plant that is designed to promote quality in production and performance.

Manufacturing overhead: The costs associated with the manufacturing process, like parts for a machine.

Manufacturing support costs: See *Indirect manufacturing costs*.

Margin of profit: See *Net profit margin*.

Marginal cost: See *Incremental cost*.

Marginal revenue: The income expected from another production line that has been completed.

Marginal utility: When a company is able to receive profit from a quality product or service or is able to write-off damaged inventory without suffering a huge loss in profit.

Mark to model: Projecting a cost for a security with information used for prior projection figures. This method can be scrutinized, because it may give a false sense of a gained profit margin for investors if the price of the investment was used when the stock yield was higher.

Mark-up: When a seller will increase the cost of an item to reach what the current market value is. For example, a shirt is listed for $5 but is selling at a competitor's store for $15. A seller may increase the price to $7 to increase the market value of the item.

Mark-up cancellation: When a seller decides not to increase the price of items based on demand of the consumers.

Markdown cancellation: When a vendor keeps a price the same based on the demand of the consumers.

Markdown: To decrease the amount of a price of an item to attract consumers.

Market interest rate: See *Effective interest rate*.

Market portfolio: Involves investments that a carry a high risk on a return rate.

Market risk premium: The measurement of how much profit will be recognized after the risk factor has been taken away.

Market share: The amount of sales a company records compared to the total amount of sales in the company's industry sector. For example, the automobile industry total sales compared to a portion of what Ford Motor Company has sold.

Market trend: When the trading market responds to the ups and downs of the prices associated with investments and securities. The terminology that applies to a market trend is "bull" or "bear."

Marketable securities: The basic investment types — bonds and stocks that are available on the trading market.

Matching rule: The duty of an accountant to try to place an income transaction with an expense transaction.

Materiality: An accountant must test accounting systems against one accounting rule at a time.

Materials inventory: A compilation of the supplies that are needed to produce or manufacture a product or service.

Materials price variance: See *Standard cost system.*

Materials quantity variance: See *Standard direct materials cost.*

Materials usage variance: See *Standard direct materials cost.*

Medicare tax: Part of the FICA tax, this tax is calculated based on an employee's wages. The current rate is 1.45 percent paid by an employee with the employer matching 1.45 percent. Medicare tax paid is 2.9 percent.

Memo entry: A transaction that does not increase or decrease the total on a balance sheet. This transaction is used for stock splits.

Merchandise inventory: The amount of products or services that have not been sold and will stay on a company's books.

Merger: The combination of two corporate entities to form one major corporation.

Mid-point convention: A company may acquire an asset during the accounting period, but it will be recognized within a certain time of the year.

Management Information System (MIS): This term refers to a company's automated system of managing information about manufacturing and technology departments.

Miscellaneous expense: Costs that are grouped together on a balance sheet because of a lower monetary value, like meals or ticket prices.

Mixed costs: When an asset is both tangible and intangible, there are different amounts to be allocated to an account. For example, mileage for a company owned vehicle.

Mixed expenses: When the cost of both a tangible and intangible asset must be allocated to an account, the charge must be broken down to reflect both assets. For example, salary for a salesman is allocated to one account, whereas the price for gas for the sales-man's car is allocated to another account.

Modified ACRS: This method replaces the original "acceler-ated cost recovery system." All depreciable assets must utilize MACRS if the assets have been utilized after 1986.

Modified book value: When income and expenses are changed from actual value to current market value.

Modified cash basis: With the combination of cash and accrual accounting systems, a company will record revenue on short-term investments when it happens, and revenue on long-term investments not due will be allocated to the next year's accounting period.

Monetary asset: A valued instrument that holds a set price amount, like cash.

Monetary unit assumption: The current value of money that is believed to be at a constant fixed price.

Money market account: A place where money for investments can be allocated under an interest-bearing account.

Mortgage bond: When a bond is used to obtain a loan to pay for real estate.

Mortgage loan payable: Transactions involving principal interest payments are recorded throughout the accounting period on the balance sheet. If the principal is unpaid at the end of the accounting period, the balance is transferred to the next accounting year.

Mortgage loan: Using the security of another loan, a borrower will try to obtain another loan to pay off an outstanding amount.

Mortgage: An obligation where a borrower pays an amount to obtain rights on a property.

Moving average: When a purchase is made, the amount of inventory sold is changed. Each time this happens, the amount changes.

MTA index: This represents the list of treasury stocks on the market for a 12-month period. The amounts are based on prior year figures and current market values.

Multicollinearity: The measurement of a dependent variable existing with two different independent variables.

Multiple-step income statement: A document that has different lines that total the same amounts on a balance sheet.

Municipal bond: A security offered by cities and municipal agencies. These bonds usually carry a tax-free clause from the state in which the bond was issued.

Mutual fund cash-to-assets ratio: How many mutual funds have been invested that can be converted to cash. If the ratio is too high, investors are buying and the fund manager cannot account for all the transactions. If the ratio is low, then the fund manager encourages investors and predicts a higher stock yield based on market prices.

CHAPTER 16

DEFINITIONS

NASDAQ (National Association of Securities Dealers): This computer-driven system is used by brokers and traders who need up-to-date information on the largest trading markets.

NASDAQ other: Not listed on NASDAQ or not quoted, this system keeps tabs on certain bids and offers.

National Association of Accountants (NAA): This group handles the management of non-certified accountants. The group formed the Institute of Management Accountants.

National Society of Accountants (NSA): An organization that offers membership to accountants who work in small accounting practices or businesses. Members perform all types of accounting services: general accounting, tax, estate planning, and auditing.

Natural accounts: These items are listed as regular expenses. An example of a natural account is the purchase of a desk for an employee.

Natural business year: Instead of a calendar year, a company may use this for its fiscal year. This is generally a 12-month term based on the start date of business operations.

Natural classification: This is a classification of costs that centers on the disclosure and reason for the expense of the item.

Natural resources: Assets that are associated with man-made or environmental materials, like gas or oil.

Near-cash assets: Items that can be transferred to cash quickly, such as rent income.

Negative amortization: When the borrower pays less then the actual amount of interest that is owed to the lender.

Negative cash flow: The cash outflow or expenses in a certain time frame is higher then the cash inflow of the same time frame.

Negative contributor: An action or process that devalues an asset.

Negative goodwill: Assets that are acquired, fairly valued, and go beyond the limit of acquisition. This will affect transactions listed on the balance sheet.

Negative pledge clause: A contract or agreement that the borrower holds if the company issues stocks or bonds that have a negative effect on the shareholders.

Negative working capital: When up-to-date liabilities are in excess of up-to-date assets.

Negligence: The failure to act responsibly toward any other person.

Negotiable instrument: A signed and transferable document that promises to pay a set amount of money to the bearer at a later date or on demand.

NET 10/30: Payment terms on an invoice. On a net 10, the net amount is due within 10 days of the date on the invoice. A net 30 would be within 30 days, and so on.

Net accounts receivable: The total amount of debit in the up-to-date assets account and accounts receivable credit balance in the allowance for doubtful accounts.

Net adjusted present value: The amount an asset is worth after the cost of the present value is deducted.

Net after tax gain: The profit recognized after tax payments have been deducted.

Net asset value: The value of assets minus the value of liabilities.

Net assets basis: The difference of net assets over shares issued.

Net assets: The total amount of assets with the total amount of liabilities subtracted.

Net book value: The amount of income versus expenses of the company. It represents money coming in and out of a company.

Net capital: The value of a company after non-liquid assets are deducted from revenue.

Net carrying amount: See *Net book value.*

Net cash flow change in cash: The difference between the cash at the beginning of the year to cash at the end of the year.

Net cash flow from financing activities: See *Cash flow from financing activities.*

Net cash flow from investing activities: See *Cash flow from investing activities.*

Net cash flow from operating activities: See *Cash flow from operating activities.*

Net cash flow: See *Cash flow.*

Net contribution: The amount remaining after all necessary deductions.

Net credit sales: How much the amount of total sales was after credit card purchases and returns were deducted from total sales.

Net current assets: Current liabilities subtracted from current assets.

Net debt: Combining short-term loans and long-term loans, minus cash and cash equivalents, which equals the net debt.

Net earnings: The total earnings minus total expenses.

Net income available for common stock: The amount of revenue a company reports after tax and dividend payments are deducted from total income earned.

Net income from continuing operations: A document outlining how much a company has in revenue after expenses are deducted.

Net income from discontinued operations: A document outlining the revenue portion for a company that will no longer continue operating a department within the company.

Net income multiplier: The amount an asset is worth calculated over the amount of time it takes for the asset to produce income.

Net income: Total revenue minus costs and expenses.

Net interest income: This amount reflects interest received on income subtracted by interest taken on expenses.

Net interest margin: A measure of interest received for income paid out on liabilities.

Net investment: The amount of a company's total securities after depreciation expenses have been deducted.

Net leases: When a tenant has to cover the rent and other expenses associated with the property. Other expenses can include maintenance fees and insurance costs. Two types of net leases are double net or triple net leases.

Net liquid assets: The amount of valued instruments that are easily converted to cash after operating expenses are deducted from total income.

Net loss: When the amount of operating expenses exceeds the total amount of revenue.

Net margin: The relation of net profits to income received from any source in a business. A percentage is calculated to find out how much profit was earned.

Net method of recording accounts payable: When a discount is taken off of a sales price, the amount of discount is allocated to accounts payable in the current accounting period.

Net of taxes: This simply means "after taxes," when all adjustments have been considered.

Net operating income: Income taxes and interest are not considered in this calculation when the company reports to net income. If the amount is a positive balance, it is considered a net income.

Net operating income: See *Earnings before interest and taxes (EBIT)*.

Net operating loss: When expenses outweigh reported income for that year.

Net operating margin: See *Net profit margin.*

Net operation profit after taxes: When a company has recorded no debt after calculating net income.

Net patient revenue: In health care administration, this is calculated by subtracting expenses from inpatient and outpatient revenue services.

Net pay: See *Gross pay.*

Net payoff: The amount of revenue recognized on securities minus operating expenses.

Net payroll payable: The amount that is owed for an employee's wages in a balance sheet account.

Net present value rule: If the net present value is calculated above zero, the investment should be considered a profitable value. If it is less than zero, the investment is considered worthless.

Net present value (NPV): The present value of cash inflows and cash outflows. This method is used to determine if something is profitable for the company.

Net profit margin: This tells how much profit a business or company makes for every dollar it makes in revenue and sales.

Net profit: The amount of cash received from cash reimbursed is calculated to see if there is a profit or loss for a certain period.

Net purchases: The cost of goods purchased after subtracting the credit balance for returns, discounts, and allowances from the debit balance in the purchase account.

Net quick assets: Valued instruments considered easily converted to cash after operating expenses are deducted.

Net realizable capital gain per share: The value of an investment after an increase in revenue has been recognized. The calculation is capital gain or loss over the number of shares the company holds.

Net realizable value (NRV): The amount a company recognizes after a company sells off an asset. The amount does not include depreciation expenses.

Net receivables: The amount recorded by the company that represents the money to be repaid without the costs of outstanding debts.

Net revenue: Gross total minus any returns and any other negative revenue.

Net sales: Also referred to as "gross sales," this is the total amount of income without the inclusion of returns, allowances, and discounts.

Net surplus: The amount of revenue recognized after certain operating expenses have been deducted. The operating expenses include tax and dividend payments.

Net tangible assets per share: The amount of revenue recognized that deals with a company's holdings in preferred stock. The amount of revenue is based on how much profit is calculated over the number of shares a company holds.

Net tangible assets: See *Book value*.

Net working capital: See *Current capital*.

Net worth: Subtracting total liabilities from total assets for a business, company, or individual. Net worth is sometimes called net liabilities.

Net yield: How much profit will be recognized on an investment after management costs have been deducted. Management costs include fees and commissions for fund managers and tax payments associated with the management of the investment.

Net-to-net lease: This agreement is that the renter pays a portion of everything — rent, taxes, insurance, and maintenance fees.

Net: The amount that remains after all deductions.

Netback: The total cost that is connected to bringing crude oil to the marketplace and the revenues from all the products that are generated from it. This term only applies to companies who are oil suppliers.

Netting: A way of reducing credit, settlement, and other risks of financial contracts when combining obligations to accomplish a reduced net obligation.

Neutrality: Economic indicators and real output are not influenced by the changes in the money supply. Money would be neutral.

Next-in, first-out cost assumption: See *FIFO method.*

Nexus: A means of connection, or a link, tie, connected group, or series between things, persons, or events. This is used to bring accounting procedures together for the entire business operation. For example, when a business operates in different locations, there must be a link to each location's requirements for reporting taxes and income.

NFP accounting standards: These standards are regulated by the Financial Accounting Standards Board (FASB) and the Government Accounting Standards Board (GASB).

NIFO: See *FIFO method.*

No-par value capital stock: A stock certificate issued without a stated value printed on it.

Nominal accounts: In accounting, these temporary accounts are closed at the end of the fiscal accounting period.

Nominal capital: The full amount of shares issued by the company.

Nominal dollars: The amount of income without adjustment for inflation.

Nominal interest rate: The rate of interest before adjustment for inflation.

Nominal ledger: This journal has the list of the company's nominal accounts.

Nominal value: The value of a share when it is issued.

Nominal: An insignificant factor that represents little cost when compared to the actual value received.

Non-manufacturing overhead costs: See *Indirect costs.*

Non-monetary asset: See *Historical cost.*

Non-trade receivable: An investment that should be converted to cash in a year after the investment had started.

Non-cash charge: See *Charge-off.*

Non-cash expense: A transaction involving the depreciation on an asset that must be recorded on a balance sheet but does not have a corresponding cash entry.

Non-cash expense: An expense that is not paid for in monetary terms, like payment for equipment on credit.

Non-cash financing and investing: Financing and investing are done without actual inflow or outflow of cash.

Non-cumulative preferred stock: An investment that does not have a set dividend payment schedule.

Non-current assets: A term used for assets that cannot be converted to cash easily and will not be for the whole year. This includes property, manufacturing plants, and equipment.

Non-current liabilities: Debts that require payment but do not reach term during the current accounting period. These obligations are carried onto future accounting periods until the term date has been reached, like a bond agreement.

Non-discretionary accrual: An obligatory transaction in the account book that has yet to be realized.

Non-discretionary: This is a mandatory requirement or compliance that does not depend upon the choice of any employee, shareholder, or business owner.

Non-equity share: A bond or stock that does not fall under the company's other equities.

Non-expendable property: Items that usually are not consumed in use and hold their identity during the period of use.

Non-expense cash disbursement: An expense of cash that does not show on the income statement. This is a legal practice in accounting. For example, the principal payment on a piece of manufacturing equipment would not appear on the income statement, because it involves a portion of the depreciation cost for the equipment.

Non-financial assets: Listed as physical assets on a company financial statement. For example, a building used for manufacturing products.

Non-fixed assets: Tangible items that are not physically attached to the building, like a shed on a rental property.

Non-fixed income: Income that changes throughout the fiscal period. For example, salary and wages change due to payments for vacation, sick pay, or health care expenses.

Non-interest bearing bond: A note without a regular interest rate; it sells at a discount and matures at face value.

Non-interest expense: Obligations that need to be met but do not incur interest, like employee wages.

Non-interest income: This represents money gained by financial institutions on investment transactions.

Non-ledger asset: Valued instruments that are not recorded in a ledger account, such as when a company has received more interest with a dividend payment.

Non-operating expense: The costs that are not part of the business functions of the company but occur in order for the company to carry out business practices, like lighting for a building.

Non-operating income/revenue: The profit recognized by a company for business activities that do not relate to the day-to-day operations. For example, merchandise sales revenue for a company promoted concert.

Non-participating: If a company needs to sell preferred stock, the stock is considered a "non-participating" company investment. The stockholder will receive the price of the current value of the stock including the cost to start the fund plus dividends that have not yet been paid.

Non-performing asset: Assets that are not producing income.

Non-professional subscriber: A person who is not affiliated with the SEC or any other securities agency. This individual engages in investment practices but has not taken the necessary steps to become an investment broker.

Non-profit organization: An organization that serves a public or other mutually beneficial need. The organization does not attempt to accumulate profit for its owners or investors.

Non-recurring: An event that is unlikely to happen again and has a negative effect on profit and loss statements in finances.

Non-trade debt: Not part of a trade; this is for interest given to an individual investor.

NOPAT: See *Net operation profit after taxes.*

Normal balance: What is expected from a particular account, based on the balance sheet of this account. Credit and debit balances are also called normal balance.

Normal costing: See *Absorption costing.*

Normal loss: An expected decline in efficient production that is unavoidable and inevitable.

Normal operating activities: The day-to-day functions of a business or corporation.

Normal profit: Profit that is expected on transactions. Normal profit is the difference between income and expenses.

Normal rate of return: In business, "normal" is any gained revenue that exceeds the cost, expenses, and taxes needed to sustain the business or an activity.

Normal spoilage: A product that has been planned or expected and is unavoidable even under the best operating conditions.

Normalized earning: A business's annual earnings over several years. It is adjusted for fortuitous gain and loss and effects of economic cycles, such as inflation.

Normative accounting theory: A theory that is not based on observation but on how an accounting process should be done. Researchers believe this theory utilizes several different approaches to end up with one correct accounting opinion. This method uses a formula to figure out income based on value, not cost.

Nostro account: Your account or money held by another entity, which is usually a bank.

Not-for-profit accounting: This type of accounting involves nonprofit companies like universities, medical institutions, and federal/non-federal government contractors. These entities must adhere to the not-for-profit (NFP) cost accounting standards.

Notarial: This refers to a task executed by a notary public, such as signatures, that certify a document's validity.

Notary public: A person who is legally certified to serve, attest, and certify non-contentious matters, signatures, and documents. The notary public does this by hand signature and certified seal for the general public. The notary public also performs certain other acts that vary in each jurisdiction.

Notes payable: An unconditional promise made by a party in a contract to repay a debt at a specified time or on demand under definite terms. Or, this can be an amount an organization owes in loans to others.

Notes receivable: A written promise or promissory note from a customer; it is a promise to pay on a definite future date.

Notes to the financial statements: These are also called foot-notes. It is additional information added at the end of financial statements to supply a full understanding of specific terms and the company's financial condition.

Not-for-profit accounting: See *Fund accounting.*

NPV: See *Net present value.*

NRV: See *Net realizable value.*

CHAPTER 17

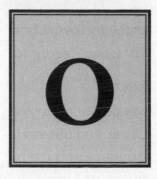

DEFINITIONS

OASDI: The former slang term utilized to describe elderly individuals, dependents of decreased persons, and insurance for disabled individuals funded by the federal government. The current name used is Social Security.

Object code: A list of the types of expenses and revenue that must be charged to an appropriate account.

Object cost: The combination of direct and indirect costs to manufacture a product or service.

Objective: In cost accounting, company personnel identify important information to report to everyone involved in the operations of the business.

Objectives in financial reporting: The responsibility of an individual who prepares a company's fiscal statements to ensure accurate information is provided to investors. Investors rely on the statements to assess a company's financial picture before making a decision to invest in that particular company.

Objectivity: To provide correct information based on the principles of GAAP.

Obligate: The act of having someone commit, bind, or compel to something by a social, legal, or moral tie.

Obligation bond: This type of investment falls under municipal bond regulations. This bond does not carry a high rate of risk, but carries a smaller profit margin.

Obligation: A payment or something owed for a special service or favor to honor a commitment to be fair in business practices.

Obsolescence: The ability to take off a bad debt or obligation without leaving a loss on the company's financial statements.

Off-the-book: A term used for transactions, such as payments or barter, that are illegally not recorded so that the transactions are hidden. Off-the-book transactions are sometimes used to hide transactions from taxation or from government regulations.

Off-balance sheet asset: Represents a resource of and entity on an item that is a positive sign of future economic value and financial position that is not recorded on the balance sheet.

Off-balance sheet financing: When companies acquire large expenditures of capital such as operating leases, joint ventures, research and developmental partnerships, but do not report these transactions on a financial statement.

Off-balance sheet liability: An item not reported on a statement as an expense but might have to be repaid at some future time. One item can include litigation proceedings.

Off-balance sheet: Recorded transactions, such as assets or debts, or other financing activity not listed on a company's financial statement.

Off-book partnership: When a company works with another company to raise capital investments. Often times, companies might do this illegally. An example of an illegal partnership is Enron.

Off-source: Used to save on cost and labor by sending out tasks to be accomplished, such as work to another provider or manufacturer.

Office equipment expense: If a company purchases or sells office equipment, the transaction must be recorded as debit or credit. This also applies to depreciation costs for the equipment.

Office equipment: Asset used for the operating functions of a company. Office equipment includes desks, chairs, computers, and light fixtures.

Office supplies expense: When a company purchases office supplies, the transaction must be recorded in the account on the balance sheet.

Officers: This term applies to the head personnel of a business or corporation. For financial operations, the person is referred to as Chief Financial Officer. For management operations, the person is referred to as Chief Executive Officer or Chief Operating Officer.

Official interest rate: The rate of interest calculated for money market investors. This rate is determined by the federal government.

Offset account: An account that reduces the gross amount of another account to obtain a net balance.

Offset: Changes to transactions that serve to compensate for differences in reported assets or liabilities.

Offsetting balance: The amount needed to keep a loan account from falling below a recommended balance.

Omitted dividends on preferred stock: See *Dividends in arrears.*

Omitted: A clause, statement, or fact that is left out or not mentioned — or included and neglected, or failed to be performed.

On account: To pay part of an obligation for products or service at one time and finish payment at a later date.

One time charge: See *Non-recurring.*

One-off: This is a single promotion that will only happen once and is recorded on the company's ledger.

One-shots: Government contracts may utilize this type of system to record expenses only to be used in that contractual period.

One-write system: This captures data at the time that transactions take place. This system is efficient and erases the need for recopying the data.

Onerous contract: An agreement that produces a product or service for a larger amount that would be the anticipated profit. An example of this is a lease contract.

Open account: An account with a nonzero credit or debit balance, a credit or charge account initiated by the creditor on the basis of credit standing, or mutually agreed-upon payment terms.

Open allotment: There is no restriction as to an amount that may be taken.

Open budget: When a company has pending transactions that will take place closer to the end of the accounting period, the budget will remain the same until each transaction has been accounted for.

Open consignment: See *Consigned goods.*

Open inflation: The rate at which costs rise due to economic trends of spending products and services.

Open item: This is found in accounting ledgers. It tracks a certain type of financial activity over a specific time period, or a scheduled commitment that does not reflect in the accounts but will be an expense at a later date.

Open market value: The price of goods and services when not controlled by cartels or government policies, but by the force of demand and supply.

Open to buy: A planning system to determine how much stock to purchase. The system utilizes projections from sales trends.

Open-book credit: A type of credit system is set up to receive merchandise with the promise to make payment.

Opening balance: After financial statements are completed, the company begins with a new amount on their balance sheet.

Opening stock: The daily price at which stocks start on the trading market.

Operating activities: See *Normal operating activities.*

Operating agreement: A legal document for the purpose of giving a detailed connection between a company and one or more of its investors in setting up and operating a program to make investments.

Operating allowance: An advance or money for costs to perform specific operations or projects.

Operating assets: These items do not expire and are used for longevity. Examples are plant materials, real estate, and research patent agreements.

Operating budget: This refers to the budgeted income (profit and loss) statement and supports documentation and schedules.

Operating cash flow ratio: This is a determination of whether current cash flow can support the amount of expenses the company has generated.

Operating cash flow: Cash that a company produces from the operations of the company. The amount of cash is calculated by deducting expenses from reported income.

Operating cost: These are recurring expenses in operating the business. The expenses can include property maintenance, taxes, and wages.

Operating cycle: Generally, an average period of time between buying inventory and receiving cash from the eventual sale of the inventory.

Operating expenditures: Day-to-day costs incurred during the normal operation of a business. These expenses include sales and supplies.

Operating expense to sales: This calculation involves how much revenue there is compared to what amount of overhead is utilized. This ratio highlights how well the company is performing.

Operating expenses budget: A revenue calculation of probable income and expenses for a set time period.

Operating expenses: Costs incurred in carrying out daily operations within the company. These costs include payroll, sales commissions, and employee benefits.

Operating exposure: To what extent a company's future cash flow will be altered by exposure to changes in the exchange rates combined with price changes.

Operating in the red: See *In the red*.

Operating income before depreciation and amortization: See *Earnings before interest, taxes, depreciation, and amortization (EBITDA)*.

Operating income: A company's net sales minus operating expenses and depreciation from gross income.

Operating interest: A form of ownership in gas and oil rights and legal rights to the revenue produced but responsible for operating cost.

Operating lease: A short-term lease compared to the useful life of an asset or equipment, for example an airplane or ship. The agreement is for a fixed monthly amount and the lessee also assumes the residual value risk of the vehicle.

Operating leverage: When a company reports a net profit, there is a degree to which the company can covert this to usable income.

Operating loss: See *Net loss*.

Operating margin: The amount of income the company can draw upon after expenses have been taken out.

Operating profit to sales: One can determine how the company turns sales into revenue by calculating income minus expenses. If the company reports a profit, this indicates how well the company is operating.

Operating profit: Income derived from deducting expenses from revenue. This amount does not include interest paid to the company from stocks and sales.

Operating ratio: In cost accounting, this is a relationship of one amount to another and measures a company's financial health, operating efficiency, and growth prospects.

Operating revenue: A company's reported income after expenses have been deducted.

Operating risk: The premise that a company could face a challenge in business operations due to economic, social, or other factors.

Operating transfer: The move of expenses from one account to another to balance operating costs.

Operational gearing: The company will maintain a position so as to not deplete their current resources and income.

Opportunity cost of revenue: Income produced to purchase more assets to yield a high rate of return.

Opportunity cost: The measurement of how one market can compete with a similar market to produce a high rate of return.

Optimal price: A typically profit-maximizing price where marginal revenue is equal to marginal price

Optimum capacity: When a company produces a great amount of goods or services with the smallest amount of cost to manufacture the product.

Optimum leverage ratio: See *Financial leverage*.

Option writer: The individual who sells investments to buyers.

Option: An agreement to purchase or sell stocks or other investments at a set value or time. If the individual does not utilize the agreement, the option is no longer valid.

Order entry: This is a process of recording an order into the company's entry system. Once an order has been entered, the company can view information about this order and make necessary changes for the entry.

Order intake: When order entries have been processed in the system, the company has acquired full responsibility to maintain the orders.

Order of liquidity: The ability to convert the most solvent assets to revenue, like cash. These items are listed on the top of a financial statement.

Order of magnitude: Its most common use is the class of scale or magnitude of any amount. The amount being scaled is 10 and the scale is the exponent. In the logarithmic scale, differences in the order of magnitude can be measured in factors of 10 or decades (meaning the power of 10; not to be confused with the term 10 years). A number is allocated to two sets of quantities. If the quantities are the same, the number has a bigger value. If the quantities are different, the number has a smaller value.

Order of permanence: Assets are listed on a financial statement based on how much the item is used.

Ordering cost: The price of materials to manufacture a product suited to a customer's order.

Ordinary annuity: See *Annuity due*.

Ordinary asset: Assets that do not meet the requirements to be listed as capital.

Ordinary course of business: A term for activities that are necessary, normal, and incidental to the business. These are common practices and customs of commercial transactions. For example, a contractor works with a financial institution to secure a loan to continue a project.

Ordinary income: Income derived from bonuses, commissions, salaries, tips, wages, and other compensations from employment.

Ordinary repairs: The cost to maintain and service equipment used in business operations.

Organization chart: The outline of a company's business formation. This outline describes each position of the company and the duties that are performed by a particular individual or department.

Organization cost: When a company decides to create a new business venture, there are fees in order to get the business running properly and legally.

Organization sustaining activities: See *Normal operating activities*.

Original cost: The price of an asset that was purchased by a company.

Original issue discount: A bond is created with a price under the par value. One example is a bond released as an interest-bearing note.

OTC (over-the-counter) bulletin board: A system that gives updated information about markets not on the NASDAQ.

Other accrued expenses payable: Transactions that represent an action that has happened but has not yet been paid for. For example, purchasing a piece of equipment that was on credit.

Other assets: See *Intangible assets*.

Other capital: See *Investment revenues.*

Other current assets: See *Non-fixed assets.*

Other current liabilities: A company's record of payments for debt obligations. An example would be dividend payouts.

Other income: Income derived from transactions not involved in daily operations of a business. For example, rent received from other business properties.

Other long-term liabilities: A company's record of payments for debt obligations that do not pay out interest on the principal amount of the loan.

Other OTC (over-the-counter): Securities not followed by the NASDAQ or the OTC that do not comply with normal trade regulations.

Out-of-cash-date: The projection as to when a company will outspend the amount of revenue that has been recorded for the accounting period.

Out-of-pocket: Paying for expenses with cash upfront and formulating the risk of not receiving payment quickly.

Outflows: The process of taking money out of an account as a transfer to another account or to pay for a product or service.

Outgo: This refers to the amount of operating expenses that have exceeded income generated.

Outlay: To put forth money to pay for products or services for personal use.

Outsource: Acquiring products or services with the use of non-company suppliers or vendors.

Outstanding checks: A document that has been given to secure payment for a product or service but has not been paid for by a financial institution.

Outstanding shares of common stock: See *Outstanding shares*.

Outstanding shares: Authorized, issued, and purchased common stocks by investors.

Outstanding: A payment that has not been received for products or services rendered.

Outturn: The year-end position in actual cash terms.

Overall market price coverage: The amount a company's investment portfolio is worth after the total amount of liabilities have been taken off the total amount of revenue earned.

Overapplied overhead costs: When a company has placed more indirect costs to a production unit in order to produce a quality product.

Overdraft: When a bank account is in a negative balance due to excessive withdrawals.

Overdraws: When an individual, business, or corporation exceeds the amount of money that is in a bank account.

Overdue: When a monetary payment for goods or services has been paid by the designated date or terms of an agreement.

Overhead absorption: Placing an amount of overhead costs to relate to the value of manufacturing a product or service.

Overhead application: See *Job costing system*.

Overhead budget: The formulation of direct and fixed labor costs for manufacturing a product.

Overhead costs: See *Manufacturing overhead*.

Overhead ratio: How much revenue it will take to meet the daily operating costs of a manufacturing cell.

Overhead variances: See *Standard cost system*.

Overhead: An operating expense for maintenance of a working environment. This can include maintaining property and taxes.

Overhead: The amount of time and money it takes to operate a business.

Overinflated: See *Inflation*.

Overleveraged: A company is unable to manage its expenses due to excessive costs.

Overstated: The act of trying to represent a fact that is not true.

Overstates: To exaggerate a profit amount to attract investors.

Overtime premium: An employee can earn 50 percent more in pay above the regular work or shift requirement. This is also known as time-and-a-half.

Overtime: Under the Fair Labor Standards Act of 1938, overtime is considered any hours that an employee works in one week that exceeds 40 hours.

Overtrading: When a firm sells stocks at a bottom-out price quickly.

Own work capitalized: When assets are created for the benefit of oneself and not for the company.

Owned receivables: A company reports payments for products or services on their financial statement.

Owner's equity: See *Stockholder's equity.*

Owner's capital account — beginning of the year: Each accounting period, the balance of an equity account does not reflect the total amount that is in the owner's equity account. The difference is based on how much revenue on investments was realized for the prior accounting period.

Owner's capital account: The value of investments minus operating expenses that are held by company stockholders.

Owner's drawing account: See *Drawing account.*

Owner's equity: The amount of assets that apply to the owner's share of the business.

CHAPTER 18

DEFINITIONS

P/E ratio (price/earnings ratio): A measurement of what the company is paying for the value of stock compared to the amount of received earnings.

Paid-in capital from treasury stock: When a corporation sells treasury stock and acquires a gain from the sale, the company will record the transaction in the stockholder's equity account on the balance sheet.

Paid-in capital in excess of par value — common stock: The amount of capital recognized after a company sells common stock. The company will record the transaction in the stockholder's equity account on the balance sheet.

Paid-in capital in excess of par value — preferred stock: The amount of capital recognized after a company sells preferred stock. The company will record the transaction in the stockholder's equity account on the balance sheet.

Paid-in capital in excess of stated value — common stock: When a company sells common stock but receives additional capital on the stock sale. The company will record the transaction in the stockholder's equity account on the balance sheet.

Paid-in capital: When a company gains income on stocks held by investors.

Paid-up capital: The amount represents the capital on stock held by the shareholders.

Paper gain (loss): An increase in the value of the stock that has not been recorded on a financial statement.

Paper: In business, this is a short-term debt security. For example, a six-month certificate of deposit.

Par value of bonds: The amount that a bond is worth on the trading market.

Par value of common stock: The amount that a share of common stock is worth on the trading market.

Par value of preferred stock: The amount that a share of preferred stock is worth on the trading market.

Par value: Maturity value or face value.

Parent company: A company that claims financial and legal responsibility of another company.

Participating preferred stock: This type can receive an increase in dividend payment above what the stock had received on the first dividend payment.

Partnership: A company where all the owners take full responsibility for income and expenses related to the business operations.

Passive activity: An activity in which you are capable of making a profit, but you do not materially participate in the activity. An example would be a CEO who runs the company but does not work in the manufacturing department.

Past cost: See *Historical cost* or *Original cost*.

Patent: A safeguard for an individual who has ownership of an invention or idea for a specified timeframe.

Pay cycle: Controls the scheduled payments that are eligible for payment in each period.

Pay: To give an individual, business, or corporation a fee for products or services that have been given or promised to another party.

Payable to shareholders: When the company allocates dividends or interest payments to stock owners.

Payable: A payment to be made.

Payables turnover: The company pays its suppliers off faster or slower than before.

Payback period: In capital budgeting, this is the amount of time it takes to break even on an investment.

Payback: The amount of money a company will receive after a project has been completed over a certain amount of time. The company will record this transaction as income earned until the money has been received in full.

Payee: The individual, business, or corporation who has been designated to receive payment.

Payer: The individual, business, or corporation who has agreed to pay another party for goods or services.

Payment due date: The date when payment should be received by the company.

Payment: The receipt of cash or other securities for products and services.

Payout period: The amount of dividends paid outlined in the terms of a bond or stock agreement.

Payout ratio: When the company gives out the amount of dividends owed to shareholders.

Payroll burden: This is the total amount needed to pay employees for a certain period of time.

Payroll taxes payable: The account on a balance sheet that tallies how much tax has been paid on behalf of the employee and employer.

Payroll variance: The difference between wages and gross pay calculated for employees.

Payroll withholdings: Amounts held from employee wages to offset income tax expenses like FICA (Federal Insurance Contribution Act tax), FUTA (Federal Unemployment tax act), Social Security, and Medicare.

Payroll: (1) The amount of wages paid to employees, (2) a company list of employees and their earned wages, and (3) the company's department that is responsible for calculating an employee's salary and benefits.

Peachtree: Commercial accounting software developed for medium- and small-sized businesses and owned by The Sage Group's software division.

Peak: The highest level of activity that has been reached in manufacturing a product or service.

PEGY ratio (PEG): The measurement of how well a stock is performing on the trading market. The ratio is calculated by taking the amount of earnings per share over the calculated annual rate of return. If the PEG is lower, the stock does not have a good rating. Conversely, the higher the rating, the better the stock is performing in the market overall.

Pension expense: The amount the company records on the balance sheet for contributions to employee pension plans.

Pension maximization: A life insurance plan that is substituted for retirement income.

Pension payable: The amount the company records on the balance sheet to allocate for the total amount of money involved in company pension plans.

Pension: Intermittent and regular benefits that are paid by an employer to an individual upon retirement from a private or government fund.

Per annum: This is defined as having to file a report once a year.

Per capita income: This represents how much each individual earns throughout the country. The amount is calculated based on variable groupings.

Per diem: A payment for regular expenses incurred for the nature of the business. An example would be meals at a restaurant with a client.

Percentage lease: A lease agreement that allows a landlord to charge rental payments based on the amount of rental units occupied.

Performance budget: Used in a governmental budget for medium- to short-range budgets.

Performance indicators: In business, these are used for evaluating specific goals and objectives.

Performing asset: Provides a positive return annually.

Period cost: General administration and selling expenses incurred and identified in an accounting period and then charged against the sales revenue in the same period.

Periodic average: A method to evaluate the cost of inventory by use of an average.

Periodic FIFO: Using the basis for the FIFO method, this evaluation is based on using the original costs associated with the inventory first and then allocating current costs to inventory that has not been sold.

Periodic LIFO: Using the basis for the LIFO method, this evaluation is based on using current costs associated with inventory that has been produced last and then allocating original costs to inventory that has not been sold.

Periodic system of inventory: When a company is still holding products or services that are ready for sale, the company will keep these on a balance sheet. Once there is a sale, the company will then transfer the amount to the financial statement.

Periodic valuation: The ability to determine costs throughout the accounting period.

Periodicity concept: The activity within the scope of an accounting period that must be recorded within the time period on a financial statement.

Permanent accounts: These areas will have an operating balance in them until the end of the accounting period, like the revenue account.

Permanent capital: The amount of profit a company recognizes with stocks and other income earned (dividends or interest payments).

Perpetual average: See *Moving average.*

Perpetual inventory FIFO: A manual or automated inventory accounting system in which inventory is accounted for in first-in, first-out basis with adjustments, delivery, and movements received being updated as they occur. For example, a company that manufactures disk players will use this method to account for inventory, because the products that were first produced will go out the door first. If there are any problems with delivery or customer satisfaction, the company can handle them as soon as the problem arises.

Perpetual inventory LIFO: A manual or automated inventory accounting system where inventory is accounted for in last-in, first-out basis with adjustments, delivery, and movements received being updated as they occur. For example, a company that takes in equipment from other companies that have been going through bankruptcy will utilize this method to move the products last acquired first before seeing what is left in inventory.

Perpetual inventory method: See *Perpetual inventory.*

Perpetual inventory: A manual or automated inventory accounting system where inventory is accounted for in a real-time basis with adjustments, delivery, movements, and receiving being updated as they occur.

Perpetual system of inventory: See *Perpetual inventory.*

Perpetuity: The influx of income at any time.

Persistent earnings: Income that continues from one year to the next.

Personal accounts: A record of amounts receivable from or payable to a person or business. These accounts are known as a sales ledger or purchase ledger.

Personal budget: An individual prepares this income and expense statement to project future income and expenses.

Personal equity: When a company retains portions of an employee's equity. This is reported on the company's financial statement.

Personal financial specialist: An accountant who is a CPA can take courses to receive a certification to handle the management of finances for individuals. These professionals can counsel individuals on financial and investing matters.

Personal loan: An amount given to an individual to use for personal benefit that must be paid off at a specified time.

Personal property: Property owned by an individual or business that is not attached to or associated with the land. Personal property is basically everything someone owns minus real property.

Personal spending: The amount of expenses an individual has accounted for during the year. This includes mortgage, car payments, medical bills, and shopping costs.

Pervasiveness of estimates: An accurate statement of cost estimates must be reported by the company.

Petty cash: Companies will keep a small amount of cash to pay for incidental expenses, such as parking fees, tolls, and office supplies, without the hassle of using checks or credit cards.

PFS: See *Personal financial specialist.*

Phantom profit: When a cash transaction has been recorded, but no cash has been received or deposited.

Physical inventory: The tally of all the assets involved in the operation of the business.

Physical life: The amount of time that a valued instrument has to perform business operations, like a piece of equipment.

Physical verification: An accountant must maintain a list of a company's inventory and assets for auditing purposes. If an asset is no longer in use, the accountant must make a notation on the balance sheet.

Piggyback: (1) Two companies take ownership of one business loan, and (2) if a company releases stock to the public, an investor can exercise the option to unload the stock at his or her discretion.

Piscan document: Adapted from 12th century Italian business owners, this method utilizes the concept that debits must equal credits.

Pitchbook: A fund manager's guidebook on how to inform potential investors about getting involved in investments and what type of investments meets the client's needs at the current time. For example, a fund manager may have specific guidelines on how to talk to clients who want to learn more about investing for retirement.

Placement: The sale of securities directly to an institutional investor, which can include banks, mutual funds, or foundations.

Plant assets: Materials — whether direct or indirect — that are involved in the manufacturing of goods or services.

Plant-wide overhead rate: The measurement of how much it will cost to produce a unit in a particular department sector of the company.

Plant: A place where a company will manufacture a good or service. A plant is considered to be a fixed asset.

Pledge: The condition of being given or held as security for a contract or payment.

Pledged accounts receivable: A business owner can utilize active accounts receivable to try to raise more capital income.

Pledged asset: An asset used to cover the costs of business expenses. The business continues to retain ownership of the asset.

Pledged revenues: The agreement to pay bondholders when a bond has been designated as a municipal bond.

Plug: When there is a discrepancy in a financial statement, this method is used to bring continuity to the finances.

Plus: A positive income increase on balance sheet. For example, a sales transaction in which income was received at the time of the sale.

Points: An additional fee paid to a lender.

Poison pill: When a merger is eminent, a company may try to reduce the value of its stock to make the company finances less desirable. For example, if a company knows it will not get FDA approval on a new drug but still needs to project a viable profit margin because of a potential merger, it will reduce the price of the stock in order to generate a quick profit.

Pool: (1) Shareholders combining their investments to counteract the prices in the market, and (2) a conglomeration of different types of stocks and bonds to maximize a high-profit return.

Pooling of interest method: A method to record equity once a merger has taken place.

Pooling of interests: When companies are going through a takeover, the assets of both companies are combined into one financial statement.

POP (point of purchase): This technique entices a consumer to think about buying an item through interesting marketing displays, like a sidewalk sale.

Portfolio risk: When an investor gets involved in stocks or bonds that can cause a decrease in return of profit.

Portfolio: The representation of investments for an individual or a company.

POS (point of sale): When an actual sale is made, the transaction is recorded as a cash or credit purchase.

Positive accounting theory: This method was initiated to better understand how accounting practices should be used.

Post balance sheet events: A transaction that is recorded after the balance sheet was prepared. This does not have a negative effect unless the transaction is recorded in the final financial statement.

Post date: When a date from the future is placed on a check or other document. This is an accepted form of payment between a business owner and a client.

Post-closing trial balance: Before an accountant will transfer revenue and expenses to the next accounting period, he or she may perform another check on the balance sheet accounts to see if there are any adjusting entries that need to be made before the financial statements are prepared.

Post-dated check: A document that has a future date inscribed so that the funds can be collected at a later time. Sometimes this is done if there are not enough funds in the account when the check is written but will be on a future date.

Post: The act of recording a transaction in the company's ledger as it takes place.

Posting: Transferring debit and credit entry amounts from a journal account to a ledger account.

Postretirement benefits: When a former employee receives compensation (other than wages) to support his or her income, because he or she are no longer working.

Practical capacity: A company must provide the best level of service without any unaffordable costs or delays.

Pre determined overhead rate: The measurement of overhead based on inventory that has already been through the manufacturing stage.

Pre-depreciation profit: Revenue recognition before depreciation expenses are deducted for the total income amount.

Pre-operating costs: Expenditures made in advance, but income has not been reported on the company's balance sheet.

Pre-tax earnings: See *Earnings before taxes (EBT)*.

Pre-tax profit margin: See *Earnings before interest, taxes, depreciation, amortization, and rent (EBITDAR)*.

Pre-tax rate of return: See *Rate of return*.

Prebilling: To submit a request for payment, although the payment is due on a later date. Medical insurance companies will submit a payment receipt before a surgery has been completed to ensure payment will be received at a later date.

Predictor ratios: This method evaluates how the company is operating at any given time.

Preemptive right: When an investor has the opportunity to acquire stock before the company issues a bid to the general public.

Preference share capital: Investors have the opportunity to receive payment first but retain no shareholder privileges.

Preferred bidder: A company may select certain investors to offer products or services through the use of contracts.

Preferred creditor: A creditor who gets paid (by law or agreement) before any other creditors.

Preferred equity: The amount of profit that is derived from a company's preferred stock and does not take into consideration profit that comes from other investments.

Preferred stock $100 par: The amount of capital received from having stock valued at $100 per share based on the par value of $100.

Preferred stock account: The place that records the amount of shares owned that are preferred stock and not common stock.

Preferred stock: A type of stock shares that pays fixed and regular interest income.

Premium on bonds payable: See *Bonds payable*.

Premium on capital stock: Shareholders acquire more dividends through the increase in the value of the stock.

Premium on common stock: The amount of excess paid on the outstanding shares of common stock that a company holds.

Premium on preferred stock: The amount of excess paid on the outstanding shares of preferred stock that a company holds.

Prepackaged bankruptcy: The ability for a company to liquidate or claim bankruptcy through a financial organization that is structured to help companies who are in financial distress.

Prepaid advertising: The costs for advertising that is paid before the actual work takes place. The company records this as an expense.

Prepaid asset: The costs for a valued instrument that have not yet taken place. For example, rent for the next month for a company building. The company will record this as an asset and an expense.

Prepaid association dues: The amount of fees paid for a company that is associated with a professional organization or management company. For example, a company paying a rental company fees for the management of a company owned property.

Prepaid dues: When a company will pay a fee for an employee to belong to a group or organization.

Prepaid expense: See *Prepaid asset*.

Prepaid expenses: Costs have been recorded for products and services acquired, but no income has been received.

Prepaid insurance: When a company pays insurance premiums for employees for the next year. This is recorded as an expense.

Prepaid rent: The amount a company pays to utilize a building, equipment, or other assets associated with business operations.

Prepayment-type adjusting entry: See *Adjusting entries.*

Prescribed security: Bond, stock, or other financial investments that have been offered by the government.

Present value factors: When a discount amount is used to project the amount of carrying value of an asset.

Present value of 1 table: The current value is multiplied by a compound interest worth 1 percent.

Present value of a single amount: See *Present value of 1 table.*

Present value of an ordinary annuity due: See *Present value of annuity due.*

Present value of an ordinary annuity: See *Present value of annuity.*

Present value of annuity due table: The list stating when annuity payments will be made on scheduled time frame.

Present value of annuity due: The discount amount of a dividend payment due at a specified time.

Present value of annuity: The discount amount of a dividend payment over the term of the stock or bond.

Present value method: The amount calculated to represent future income due to an investor.

Present value table: See *Present value of 1 table*.

Present value: See *Net Present value*.

Price ceiling: The government is responsible for setting a reasonable amount for consumers to pay for products and services.

Price earnings multiple: See *P/E ratio*.

Price elasticity: How consumers react to prices for goods and services.

Price fixing: An illegal practice that falls under the Clayton Antitrust Act of 1914. This happens when competing companies join forces to eliminate competitors. For example, the 2001 Enron scandal.

Price mixes: A price-related total of information and conditions that is submitted to the customer.

Price to book: A method used to determine and compare the business's book value to current market price.

Price to cash flow: A measure to determine how a company's income rates against the price of their stock in the current market.

Price to revenue: This method is utilized to compare the current value of stock to prior year's stock valuation. This is calculated by dividing stock price over income.

Price-earnings ratio: See *PEGY ratio*.

Price: The cost at which something is purchased.

Primary activities: See *Normal operating activities*.

Primary dealer: A select list of securities firms that have been given authorization by the Federal Reserve System to deal directly in government bonds with a central bank that controls a country's currency.

Prime brokers: Providers who offer a specific professional service aimed at hedge funds and other large institutional customers.

Prime cost method: This represents how much depreciation is calculated on fixed assets.

Prime costs: The amount of operating expenses that are involved in the manufacturing process. These amounts do not include overhead charges.

Prime rate: The universal method of charging interest on accounts at financial institutions.

Principal payment: The amount of principal paid for a loan agreement.

Principal: Defined in the accounting field as an individual who has controlling authority in a company or business.

Principles and guidelines: The rules and regulations that are enforced by the GAAP.

Principles-based accounting: This accounting method utilizes the practices set forth by the GAAP.

Prior period adjustment: See *Adjusting entries*.

Prior period: Income or expenses that were recorded in the company's previous financial statements.

Private corporation: A corporation composed of a few owners and shares that have no public market value.

Private equity: Investments that are held in securities that the company does not trade on public markets.

Private placement: Investments from stocks and bonds sales that are held by private companies. This is restricted to qualified individuals whose net worth is typically $1 million.

Pro forma financial statement: A document that is prepared to figure out future costs and income for a company for the next accounting period.

Pro forma income: The revenue amount that is projected by accountants on a pro forma financial statement.

Pro forma invoice: An agreement for a product or service with a set price and conditional terms. It states the selling price and terms offered. Pro forma invoices are frequently used as preliminary invoices with a quotation or for U.S. Customs purposes in importation.

Pro rata: Proportionately in agreement with an exactly calculable factor (as share or liability). For example, a lender will assign a pro rata for a savings account. The interest rate will be 15 percent for 12 months, which figures out to 1/15 for each month during the year.

Proceeds: Income that has been recognized because a company has received payment for business loans to individuals or from investing activities.

Proceeds: Generally in business, it is the amount of money received minus transaction costs.

Process cost system: A method of evaluating inventory based on the price of manufacturing a product or service. This system factors in manufacturing direct and indirect costs.

Process costing: In cost accounting, this process is formed by the collection of manufacturing costs by departments or by production processes.

Procurement: In business, it is obtaining goods and services.

Producer price index: This determines inflation on goods and services in the economy based on a range of pricing strategies.

Product cost: The amount it takes to produce or manufacture goods or services. An example would be the materials to produce a doll.

Product warranty cost: If a product or service becomes damaged and is returned to the company, the company will expense the cost of replacing the item or issuing a refund.

Production department: A sector of the company that is responsible for manufacturing products or services.

Production service department: A sector of the company that is responsible for maintaining the equipment and parts that are responsible for manufacturing products or services.

Production volume variance: See *Fixed manufacturing overhead volume variance.*

Profit and loss account: This is the net profit for a company once expenses have been taken out.

Profit and loss statement: A statement of revenues and expenses that show a profit or loss for the company for the fiscal year. It represents a report card of a company's activities.

Profit before taxes: A calculation of the company's income versus expenses, with the exclusion of tax payments.

Profit center: A private sector of a company that is responsible for producing and maintaining its own income and expenses.

Profit margin: See *Net profit margin*.

Profit maximization: The ability for a company to achieve a maximum profit with low operating expenses.

Profit motive: The ultimate achievement for a company to be able to generate more profit without the cost of high operating expenses.

Profit multiple: See *Operating profit*.

Profitability: In order to provide sustainability for a business, the business must generate more income to pay expenses.

Profitable: See *Profitability*.

Program budget: A budget prepared with program descriptions instead of expense line items.

Program evaluation and review technique (PERT): The method of evaluating cost and management accounting procedures as they relate to the manufacturing process. If there are any discrepancies or differences, the company makes the changes to ensure the continuing quality of manufacturing as well as increase profits.

Progressive tax: Defined as higher incomes pay a high percentage of income in taxes. A graduated tax is one example.

Projection: An estimate of future economic events that can increase or decrease the total profit margin. This can include purchase of assets and management of liabilities.

Promissory note: In accounting, this is usually just called a "note payable" or "note." This is a written agreement between two parties for a specified amount and time to be paid.

Promotional allowances: Manufacturers will offer retailers compensation for work to promote a product or service.

Proof of posting: To ensure transactions were recorded properly on a company's journals or ledgers.

Property dividend: A payment made on an investment in real estate or land development.

Property inventory: A list of a company's fixed assets, like buildings.

Proprietary: Owned by a private individual or corporation under a patent or trademark.

Proprietor: An individual who operates a business and is responsible for all financial operations of the business.

Proprietor's funds: The blending of the owner's equity and investments.

Proprietors draw: The drawing of money by the owner for personal needs. The amount is taxable based on an individual rate.

Proprietorship: See *Sole proprietorship*.

Propriety asset: Customarily, any asset or all information of customers/clients that should not be disclosed, including business and personal information.

Propriety theory: A theory that states assets and liabilities are the responsibility of the business owner.

Prospectus: This is a statement or situation that predicts the course or nature of a business.

Protest: A statement that clearly states disagreement with a payment and reserves the right to regain it later.

Provision for credit losses: An allowance set aside that is judged adequate to cover anticipated credit losses.

Provision for doubtful accounts: See *Allowance for bad debts.*

Provision: Steps taken to prepare for a contingency or need.

Provisional: An action that will serve now, and that is acceptable for the situation, but is subject to change at a later date.

Proxy: Giving an individual the right to act on behalf of another person, like signing a financial statement.

Prudence concept: An accounting concept where expenses and liabilities are recognized as soon as possible, but revenues are only recognized when realized and assured.

Public accountant: A person who has the required experience and skill in recording, maintaining, and management of accurate financial records for an individual or business.

Public corporation: A corporation created to perform or operate a governmental function. These may include municipal water companies, post offices, and hospitals.

Public debt office: Under the control of the U.S. Department of Treasury, this area is responsible for maintaining the regulations for investments.

Public funds: Money that is generated by the government to provide goods and services to the general public.

Public offering: An offer to the public to buy securities by an underwriter. This transaction must be registered by the Securities and Exchange Commissions (SEC).

Publicly traded stock: See *NASDAQ*.

Purchase account: Transactions are recorded for all inventory purchases in this account.

Purchase acquisition: An accounting method performed in any merger that is not negotiated as a pooling of interests.

Purchase agreement: A contract that outlines the terms of acquiring a good or service.

Purchase commitments: When a company has entered into an agreement to acquire a new company but no formal proceedings have taken place.

Purchase ledger: Preserves a record of goods and services that a company buys on credit.

Purchase method: This determines the fair market value of a stock in reference to actual price of the stock.

Purchase order: A written order for the supplier to ship products at a definite price; this is a legally binding contract when accepted by the supplier.

Purchase outright: To pay the full purchase price amount in cash.

Purchase requisition: An official order form used by companies when purchasing a product or service; includes the description and quantity and may include an authorized purchase.

Purchases discounts: When a sale transaction has occurred, an additional cost is taken off the original price of the item.

Purchases returns and allowances: A company policy that allows customers to return an item that was purchased if it was damaged or unused.

Purchases-net: See *Net purchases.*

Purchasing power: A consumer's ability to buy products or services based on his or her personal needs.

Pure cost: In cost accounting, this amount is based on how much inventory was priced at in previous years. This method compares present and past prices.

Push-down accounting: This method relates to a company that went through a merger with another company. Costs that have been accrued are transferred to the other company.

Push-pull strategy: This method defines how products and services leave the business and go to the clients. A client wants to buy a product (the pull), and the business (the push) will satisfy the client's request.

Put down: When a company decides to reduce its prices to compete with another company's pricing strategy.

Put option: The ability to acquire a stock and then sell the stock at a determined price at a later date.

Put warrant: A stock can be set at a determined price and the amount does not expire.

Put: The ability to sell a stock at a set price.

Pyramid selling: This method involves an individual receiving money from people who work for the company, but no goods or services are being provided. This is considered an illegal business practice.

CHAPTER 19

DEFINITIONS

Q ratio: Developed by Yale University Professor James Tobin, this is the method of evaluating a stock's performance by utilizing the status of a company's share versus the current asset value.

Qualification: The representation of an accountant's ability to perform and carry out the duties assigned by a business or corporation.

Qualified acceptance of a bill: The obligation for payment when goods or services have been provided for a fee.

Qualified accounts: Investments that are not subjected to taxes until dividends and payments are made. For example, a 403-B employee contribution plan.

Qualified dividend: This payment is subjected to the implication of taxes on generated revenue.

Qualified domestic relations order (QDRO): This document represents a decision enforced by a court that allows divorced spouses to be recipients of dividends from pension plans and stock investments.

Qualified domestic trust: The allowance for a foreign individual to receive benefits from a spouse who is considered a citizen of that country. Under this agreement, foreign individuals are entitled to receive benefits from estates, pension plans, and medical treatment. Taxes are deferred until dividends are paid.

Qualified opinion: When an auditor offers his or her statement of validity on the financial statements of the company.

Qualifying shares: The amount of stock considered for an individual to be appointed on the corporation's governing body.

Qualitative characteristics: Guidelines that an accountant must follow based on FASB rulings.

Qualitative factor: These elements highlight a company's performance. The elements include profit margin, turnover rates, and management style.

Quality assurance: The determination that a business or corporation is satisfying consumers' needs with the best goods and services.

Quality control: A company must define ways to produce the best goods or services for consumers.

Quality cost: The amount applied to producing a good or service.

Quality of earnings: Changes in the inflation rate directly affect how a stock will perform in the stock market. If the inflation rate is high, the stock market will have less of a rate of return on profit. If the inflation rate is low, the stock market will have a greater rate of return on profit.

Quantifiable: To assess the performance of a company through ratios.

Quantise: The description of a valued instrument is changed when trading exchange is different. For example, converting a piece of equipment to a dollar amount for a different market.

Quantity demanded: This is how much consumers want to receive whenever the demand is great.

Quantity discount: If a consumer purchases a large amount of products from a company, the company will offer a lower price to retain future business from the consumer.

Quantity supplied: This is how much a business or corporation produces to meet the demand of the consumers.

Quantum meruit: A Latin phrase meaning to make sure products and services are delivered based on an agreement between a supplier and a consumer.

Quarter-on-quarter: Separating an intangible asset into four equal pieces. For example, dividing ownership of a property among four people.

Quarterly report: A document outlining fiscal operations that is given to stockholders four times throughout the year.

Quarterly: The division of an item into four pieces. For example, a company's financial statement will be circulated four times throughout the year.

Quasi-loan: An agreement between individuals to pay off obligations, but with the intention to receive partial payment in the future.

Quasi-public corporation: A company that is privately owned but is regulated by the government. Employees are not compensated by the government. An example would be a federal subcontractor on a Navy contract.

Quick assets: If a company needs to generate more income, a valued instrument can be exchanged into revenue.

Quick ratio: If the current ratio is determined to be incorrect, this method is used to find out about limited assets.

Quid pro quo: From the Latin phrase that translates to "something for something," a contract that involves businesses that exchange a product between the two entities. For example, a business exchanges a patent for another business's patent.

Quorum: When a company must have a certain amount of employees to make decisions about investments.

Quota: (1) The amount a company sets as a benchmark to produce for the following year, or (2) a price set for a product or service that involves a foreign business or corporation.

Quotation: The amount of money required to purchase investments. There are different types of quotations: direct and indirect. A direct quotation is expressed in the form of dollars. An indirect quotation is listed as it would appear on the foreign market.

Quote: The amount at which a security is valued on a daily basis at the trading market.

Quoted company: A business or corporation that is listed on the trading exchange.

Quoted investments: When a bond or stock is issued, there is an understanding of how the bond or stock will be honored at maturity.

Quoted share: The financial investment a shareholder has in a business or corporation.

CHAPTER 20

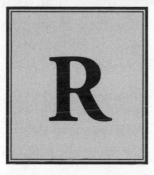

DEFINITIONS

Rate of economic growth: This is calculated to determine the economic status throughout the year.

Rate of exchange: The way in which money can be transferred from one exchange to another.

Rate of inflation: This measurement is influenced by how high or low the prices of goods and services move throughout the economy.

Rate of return: The amount an investor expects to gain from his or her investments.

Ratio analysis: A method to evaluate the quality of a company's manufacturing process based on a cost system.

Ratio: The relationship of different amounts of products or goods to how much is produced.

Raw materials inventory: See *Direct materials.*

Real account: An area that appears on a balance sheet for every accounting period, like cash.

Real assets: A valued instrument that is intangible. For example, large quantities of silver held by the company.

Real capital: See *Operating income.*

Realization: When assets are converted to cash or securities.

Reasonable test: A measurement to determine the validity of an action or process.

Receipts: A way to determine if a product or service was recorded as a payment.

Receivable days: The length of time given by a company to receive payment for goods or services.

Receivable turnovers: The rate a business or corporation receives payment for goods or services and how long unpaid obligations continue to accrue on the balance sheet.

Recession: The loss of financial stability in a country's economical status.

Reciprocal services method: When two departments perform the same duties within the company, there will be identical charges made for both departments.

Recognize: (1) To allocate or associate income or expenses to balance sheet accounts, or (2) the point when a transaction becomes part of the business.

Recompense: To pay for expense incurred out of a legal decision or action.

Reconciliation of a bank statement: See *Bank reconciliation.*

Record date: When a transaction is allocated on a general ledger or balance sheet.

Record: The accounts for revenue and liabilities listed on a company's financial statement.

Recoup: Payment to cover costs associated with legal claims.

Recourse loan: An individual can be charged with repayment of an obligation by a financial institution if the individual defaults on a loan.

Recovery: To try to reclaim stability in business practices during a bad economy.

Red flag: (1) The warning sign that indicates there is a problem with a stock or bond. Investors need to be wary of this distinction, because it represents the poor performance or quality of a stock or bond, or (2) when illegal or fraudulent activity is found within a business or corporation.

Red herring: This is an agreement to discuss the offerings of a newly formed corporation. It is meant to introduce a new corporation to potential investors and brokerage firms before stocks or bonds can be traded, and it has to be started by the SEC.

Red ink: When a business or company's operating expenses exceed revenue and the balance sheet will reflect a negative number.

Redeem: A payment received by stockholders.

Redeemable bonds: A company may exercise an option to recall bonds before the bond is set to mature.

Redeemable share: A company can recall shares before the shares expire.

Redemption date: The time a stock or bond takes to reach maturity.

Redemption fee: This cost is associated with the recall of a mutual fund. An individual will incur these costs during the recall transaction.

Redemption price: The amount an investor receives, but this does not include payments of dividends.

Redemption: The amount of payment given to a stockholder after the sale of a stock or bond. The payment must be paid in a reasonable amount of time to be considered a redeemable stock or bond.

Rediscount: If a loan payment has already been reduced, a financial institution may reduce the payment amount further to satisfy the loan quicker.

Redlining: The method of discriminating against a particular group of people. In the 1960s, Northwestern University Professor John McKnight challenged this practice. McKnight felt this was an outright attack on people just by reason of where they lived. He coined the term when speaking of the practice of marking areas on a map with red pen to delineate where a bank would not invest.

Reduction option loan (ROL): This instrument uses different types of loans to give a consumer an affordable interest rate. For example, a mixed mortgage loan with two different rates.

Refinancing: An option given to an individual to repay a current loan with a different type of loan that will cover the payments.

Reflation: To help boost a fledging economy, an agreement is made to lower the current interest rate and try to increase demand to counteract the effects of inflation. For example, offering reduced interest rates on home-equity loans.

Refund: If an individual is overcharged by a business, the business will give a payment back to an individual.

Refurbish: To recycle a product for a new use or purpose.

Region: A place where individuals work, live, or participate in recreational activities.

Regional bank: A financial institution that operates in a specified location. For example, a community bank that serves customers living in a rural area.

Regional exchange: A trading market located where the predominant groups of businesses or companies reside and where they operate. For example, the traded company in Pennsylvania would operate out of Philadelphia.

Regional fund: An investment that is found only where the business or company is located. This fund is mostly made up of foreign entities so individuals can broaden their investments on a financial portfolio.

Register: To assign income and expenses to the correct ledger account.

Registered investment adviser: An individual who is a member of the Securities and Exchange Commission and is able to provide financial and investment management strategies for individual and business investors.

Regressive tax: This represents a tax when an individual's income increases. One type of regressive tax is social security tax. This tax applies only to a limited amount and does not increase after reaching the amount.

Relative sales value method of allocating cost: See *Average cost method.*

Relevant assertions: An accountant's responsibility to ensure a business or corporation is using due diligence in business operations.

Relevant cost: An amount that has been allocated to an income or expense, which can be adjusted to meet the actual price of what was charged by the company.

Relevant range: The timeline of when a company will perform a business that provides certain goods or services.

Reliability: Accurate information on business activities must be given to company management.

Remit: To make payment for goods or services rendered.

Remittance: The action of giving a person payment through a financial instrument, like a money order for a product from a supplier.

Rent expense: The amount to be paid on a lease agreement. This amount is usually based on a per-month basis.

Rent expense/income: The amount paid to a property owner for a leased property. This amount is also considered income, because it is money paid on a leased property. The amount is recorded in both an income and expense account.

Reorder point: The time when an inventory supply needs to be replenished.

Repairs and maintenance expenses: The upkeep cost of machinery and equipment for the use of business operations or the upkeep of rental properties. For example, fixing a copier or fax machine and servicing the light fixtures in an apartment building.

Replacement cost accounting: A way to assign depreciable value to reclaim operating costs for equipment no longer in service.

Replacement cost: The amount to receive an item in return for the one that was damaged or is no longer in service.

Replacement value: The cost allocated to gain a new asset equal to the one that has to be taken out of service.

Replenish: To rebuild the amount of money that is supposed to be available for petty cash funds. For example, if $50 was taken from the petty cash fund in one month, then in the following month, $50 should be put back into petty cash.

Requisition: An agreement that a business will provide a customer with a good or service.

Required rate of return: The amount a company needs to earn on investments held.

Research and development costs: Expenses related to the inception and production of new products that have not been sold or released by a company. These costs are based on projected values.

Residual: The amount recognized after expenses have been deducted from the total income.

Residual standard deviation: The difference between what is noted as an actual cost or as a projected cost of an asset or liability.

Residual value: The predicted cost of an asset after depreciation has been deducted from the actual cost of the asset.

Restatement: (1) If a company's financial statements were changed, the company will issue a document to highlight the changes that were made, or (2) the announcement of money from one exchange to another exchange.

Restricted accounts: An area that holds revenue that will be used for future purchase of an investment or asset. For example, money set aside for the purchase of a new building.

Restricted cash: Money that has been earmarked for certain purposes. For example, the purchase of a bond security.

Restricted retained earnings: Profit from investments that has not been derived from dividend payments.

Restructuring charge: When a company goes through a change in the operations of a business, a fee is required for this transaction. This does not affect a shareholder's stake in the company, because this fee is only incurred one time in a financial statement.

Retail method: The determination of how much profit is realized in reference to the amount of goods and services sold.

Retained earnings: The amount of income a company recognizes on the balance sheet after dividends have been paid to investors.

Retained earnings statement: See *Statement of stockholder's equity*.

Retention rate: The projected amount of how much return a company will carry on to the next accounting period. It is not included in a dividend payment.

Retirement of assets: When a company decides to no longer use equipment for business operations. The company will not receive any profit from taking the equipment out of service.

Retirement of bonds: When a company decides to purchase bonds that have already been issued by another company.

Returned check: See *Bounced check.*

Return on assets: See *Return on investment.*

Return on average common stockholder equity: See *Return on stockholder's equity.*

Return on capital (ROC): The measurement of a company's ability to provide a profit to the stockholders while maintaining operating expenses.

Return on equity: This is calculated by using income divided by equity.

Return on invested capital (ROIC): The company's ability to utilize generated income from investments to maintain a low level of operating expenses.

Return on investment (ROI): The profit received by an individual investing in a financial instrument like a stock, bond, or mutual fund.

Return on net assets (RONA): The amount a company generates in income for the year. If the company reports a high amount, the profit return is significant for investors.

Return on sales: The amount of income recognized for sales made during the year.

Return on stockholder's equity: The amount a company recognizes from income on investments over the amount of equity stockholders held for the accounting period.

Return on total assets (ROA): The amount of revenue based on the company's assets. This does not include payments of interest dividends.

Revenue bonds: A security used to fund improvement projects like highways and buildings. This can also represent a municipal bond.

Revenue center: A group set up within a company that is responsible for managing income.

Revenue expenditure: These amounts are recorded when the expense occurs. An example is maintaining the controls on plant equipment.

Revenue leverage: An individual applies for a loan to pay off obligations on another loan.

Revenue recognition: When the amount of income is recorded on the company's financial statements.

Revenue ruling: Managed by the Internal Revenue Service (IRS), these methods aid businesses or corporations in identifying how the allocation of income and expenses should be handled.

Revenue sharing: When an individual, business, or corporation must pay taxes on income earned to other state and local government agencies. For example, a baseball player for the Philadelphia Phillies must pay city and wage taxes when he plays in Miami, Florida.

Revenue: This is a positive influx of assets due to offering or exchanging products or services. If the company utilizes a credit method, the transaction is allocated as money to be received at a later date.

Risk adjusted return: The degree of risk associated with how much profit will be received.

Risk rate: How a stock or bond is evaluated based on the level of risk.

Risk: The degree of uncertainty when engaging in a potentially unreasonable manner or activity. For example, getting involved in a new business venture.

Rollover: When an investor has accumulated interest in an investment and wants to transfer it to another related investment strategy. For example, when an employee transfers money from one IRA to another IRA.

Royalty: Income received by an individual for his or her involvement in a professional project, like a writer who receives a payment for a story in a book.

Rule: To carry out a regulation imposed by a governing board. In accounting, this applies to the GAAP.

Run rate: The company's projected profit is examined to make investment decisions for the next year. An example would be a pool installer company that looks at profits during the winter in the Northeast.

CHAPTER 21

DEFINITIONS

Safeguarding of assets: The method of protecting and maintaining a company's daily business operations.

Safety margin: To assure the quality of company investments for a shareholder.

Safety shares: Stock that is in reserve for a company to use in case the company experiences a financial loss in operations.

Salary: See *Gross pay*.

Salary and fringes: See *Employee fringe benefits*.

Sales allowance: A lower price is offered for products that were manufactured and considered to be damaged or improperly made. For example, a T-shirt with a logo printed on the arm instead of on the front of the shirt.

Sales and leaseback agreement: When two companies are involved in the sale of a property, but one of the companies decides to continue to conduct business at the property. The agreement defines terms and conditions of the sale.

Sales budget: A projection of how much a business will generate in profit for the year. This is not a true form of determination for profit margin.

Sales commission expense: A company records this transaction when a stock or bond has been sold. This transaction is included on the financial statement.

Sales discount: When a company offers a reduced price to consumers who make payments on time.

Sales forecasting: An estimation of how much a company will generate income based on sales.

Sales journal: The area where purchases are recorded before the transactions are considered accounts receivable.

Sales ledger: The document where daily income on products or services sold is recorded.

Sales mix analysis: The measurement of how a company will maintain a profit when there are several different products or services to consider.

Sales return: When a consumer is not satisfied with a product and expects to receive the full amount paid for the product.

Sales returns and allowances: The account where a company records a return made by a customer.

Sales tax: The amount attached to the purchases and payments of goods and services.

Sales to cash flow ratio: The measurement of how income is compared to the amount of transactions recorded.

Sales: The act of providing a good or service in return for payment.

Salvage value: The amount that is calculated once a piece of equipment is no longer used in business operations.

Savings account rate: The amount of interest that an account holder will receive based on a set rate.

Scrap value: The amount that is calculated when a company has leftover material that can be used for processing. This amount is written off on the factory overhead expense.

Scroll: The earliest format in recording business transactions.

Search: To find an area identified by an auditor that needs to be reviewed for quality and accuracy.

Secret reserve: An amount not identified to anyone involved in the process of bidding on stocks or bonds except for the individual who is issuing the option to buy.

SEC filing: Businesses or companies that are trading on the public markets must file a financial statement with the SEC.

Secondary activities: When a company performs business operations that are outside of the normal business practices. For example, a litigation case against the company for a broken stairwell that led to an accident inside the company's headquarters.

Secured basis: A business owner or company will offer assets as a way to obtain a loan.

Secured bond: An investment that involves collateral.

Secured creditor: An institution that holds a lien on a person's personal property until the investment is paid off.

Secured liability: An amount to be received as payment on held obligations. For example, a piece of equipment is used as collateral until a loan has been paid off.

Security: An asset that can be sold to meet the financial obligations of a defaulted individual, like real estate.

Securities and Exchange Commission (SEC): This organization oversees the transactions of publicly traded markets. The SEC utilizes FASB to watch over a company's fiscal practices.

Seed money: Income used towards the start up of a new business or company.

Segment: The ability to divide a product into pieces during the manufacturing process.

Segment margin: The measurement of how well a single department is performing as it relates to the whole operations of a business or company.

Segregated account: The amount of investments that are recorded in a different account on the balance sheet.

Self-balancing self-constructed asset: These valued instruments receive an additional boost of income from interest accrued on each asset.

Self-employed income: Wages earned by individuals who are not salaried employees of a business or company. For example, an individual who is a content writer is hired by a publishing company to produce a book in a limited amount of time.

Sequential: Income and liabilities are recorded as transactions in alphabetical order.

Sequential sampling: Transactions listed in alphabetical order are measured to see if income minus expenses equals a total profit.

Serial bonds: A company issues several bonds at the same time, but each bond will mature on a different date.

Short account: Transactions are recorded based on financial investments being sold at a bottom price.

Short interest: The cost associated with financial investments being sold at a bottom price but not recorded as interest income.

Short sale: If a business or corporation is trying to get out from underneath financial woes, the option to sell off property quickly without claiming bankruptcy.

Short-debt ratio: The measurement of how much a company can pay off operating expenses in the current accounting period.

Short-term asset: See *Current assets*.

Short-term debt: The amount a company is carrying in operating expenses on a financial statement.

Short-term investments: Financial instruments that expire in a very short amount of time — usually less than a year.

Short-term liability: See *Current liabilities*.

Shortage costs: The price that is allocated when inventory is low.

Shrinkage: The difference between inventory presented on the company ledger compared to inventory actually visible within the business operations, due to something like an employee stealing company supplies.

Sight draft: Money must be repaid quickly when a customer presents this document to a business or corporation.

Significance testing: The method of figuring out the validity of a manufacturing process.

Significant: The measurement of how well a company performs against competitors.

Simple capital structure: A stock option that can be changed easily into a common stock.

Simple interest: Investors can use this method to determine how much interest will be returned on a stock or bond. The calculation is based on taking the interest rate times initial principal, times the length of the security.

Simple rate of return: The evaluation of how much profit is made in relation to how many products were produced for that year.

Simple regression: This process evaluates the sales projections for the upcoming accounting period.

Simple yield: The amount of interest received based on the current cost of a stock or bond.

Single-entry bookkeeping: The process of recording transactions on one side of a business statement or ledger.

Single-step income statement: An easy way to track income and expenses with one-line items and one total at the bottom.

Sinking fund: The company will exercise the option to repurchase funds that are due to expire.

Sinking fund method of depreciation: The company will allocate a cost to the value of the fund before the company reissues the stock or bond to the general public.

Skimming price: The process of setting an inflated cost to attract consumers. Once the need for the product has diminished, the company will bring the cost back down to the regular value of the product.

Slack: When a company is not moving inventory too quickly but is doing nothing about it to resolve the issue.

Slack path: The measurement of the ability to move inventory with a little bit of time required.

Social accounting: This method utilizes the basic principles of accounting in social aspects of economics. The social aspects include environment and medical accounting systems.

Social audit: A measurement of how businesses and companies that use a social accounting system report income and expenses on a financial statement.

Social impact system: This document highlights how companies in the service industry are making a difference with the development of new products and technologies.

Social Security tax: This tax was created under the Federal Insurance Contributions Act (FICA). The amount taken from a contributor's earnings covers support for retired workers, those on disability, and individuals who are entitled to survivorship benefits, which provide financial support for individuals of a deceased family member who was the primary breadwinner.

Soft landing: When there is a greater risk of going into an economic depression but the economy is kept afloat despite bad financial conditions.

Sole proprietor: When an individual serves as primary and only owner of a business or company. In this type of ownership, all assets and liabilities are the responsibility of the owner.

Solvent: A business or corporation is able to pay its operating expenses.

Source document: A record of a reported transaction. This transaction can be found in different areas, like receipts, checks, and registers.

Sources of evidence: A valuable tool to track income and expenses reported on a balance sheet. Sources include ledger and journal accounts.

Spam: Inaccurate advertising media floated around the Internet.

Special assessment funds: Accounts set up for expenses incurred for capital projects.

Special audit: An assessment based on a report by an auditor that requests further analysis of a business practice.

Special journal: A record of transactions that serve a specific purpose in a business or company. For example, a cash accrual journal.

Special miscellaneous account: An area where money can be put in to absorb costs that were incurred by capital losses.

Special purpose entity: This business structure allows companies to operate smaller business operations without the hassle of a large financial risk.

Special report: A document certified by an auditor that evaluates how a company has complied with the GAAP.

Special revenue fund: An account with an insignificant amount of profit reported on a financial statement.

Special situation: An issue that requires a company to decide to sell off shares. For example, if two companies combine their business operations into one entity.

Special-order decisions: When a company tries to figure out if it is worth keeping products that are undervalued.

Special-purpose financial statement: A document outlining an agreement that an investor will not use money for loan payments to purchase investments.

Specialist: An individual who is qualified to carry out the duties and responsibilities in the field of accounting.

Specialized industry: An individual engages in educational studies to obtain a job in a specific area, like accounting.

Specific identification: The process of allocating a price to the amount of inventory on hand.

Specific price index: A dollar amount that is assigned to a product or service, depending on the current economic status.

Specific price-level change: See *Specific price index*.

Speculation: The act of increasing the value of a stock by projecting the costs of new investments.

Spending variance: See *Standard cost variance*s.

Spin-off: When a company has gone through a merger, the company's current stockholders will be granted the option to acquire stock from the new company.

Split-off: When a piece of a company is sold off, the stock is converted into shares of the new company.

Split-off point: The moment inventory becomes an actual cost on a company's financial statement.

Spoilage: The by-product of the manufacturing process that cannot be used again for manufacturing or for sales.

Spot price: The exact value of a bond or stock on the current market.

Spontaneous assets: These tangible items increase as a direct result from greater business activity, like payment for service that was already completed.

Spreadsheet: A document that is used to track income and expenses for a business or corporation.

Staff auditor: An individual who performs assessments and valuations of a company's financial status. This person can be either employed by the company or by an outside accounting practice.

Staff authority: This unit provides counseling on financial matters to the company's management personnel.

Stand-alone cost method: The measurement of how much cost is involved in the production process in relationship to how many units are produced.

Stand-alone revenue allocation: The process of allocating a cost to the amount of products or services generated.

Standard accounting practice: See *Generally accepted accounting principles.*

Standard bill of materials: The form that describes how much payment will be received for products or services sold by a business or company.

Standard cost system: An amount is allocated for goods or services that are produced and included in the company's inventory.

Standard deduction: This is available to every taxpayer who wishes to deduct business and personal expenses. The deduction is based on the filing status of the taxpayer.

Standard deviation: To determine how efficient a company's production is. This is based on the company's assets and the company's projected rate of return.

Standard direct material costs: This is calculated by using the cost, times the amount of the product. For example, if the cost of material is $3.50 per unit, multiplied by 9 products, the direct material would equal $31.50.

Standard factory overhead costs: This represents factory costs (variable and fixed) to be accounted for the company in the following year.

Standard hours allowed: The amount of time it takes to produce a quality product or service.

Standard labor rate: The amount of hours worked to manufacture a product.

Standard material rate: The cost that is allocated to the amount of supplies that will be used in the production of a product.

Standard of comparisons: To evaluate the amount of costs to produce a product in comparison to how many units are produced.

Standard opinion: See *Qualified opinion*.

Standard-quantity allowed: The amount of inventory a company keeps in inventory without compromising operating liabilities.

Standard: The idea of what is an acceptable form of payment for goods or services rendered.

Start-up costs: The amounts associated when a business or company has been newly formed.

State of unemployment compensation: When an employee is laid off, the individual may be entitled to collect support from the state where they live. This support offers compensation until the individual is able to find another job.

Stated capital: The amount of stock a company has issued.

Stated value: The amount of shares reported on the company's financial statements.

Statement of account: This document includes a company's financial information as well as tax information.

Statement of affairs: The document that outlines income and expenses for a company to report a profit or loss.

Statement of cash flows: An assessment of how much cash, business costs, and investments were generated by the company.

Statement of cash receipts and reimbursements: This document shows the relationship of how much income was received and how much income was given to cover operating expenses.

Statement of goods manufactured: This document outlines how many products were produced in relation to how much income was generated.

Statement of operations: See *Profit and loss statement*.

Statement of realization and liquidation: The document highlights the amount of shares held by the company and how much the company would need to issue in order to generate income if financial crisis is encountered.

Statement of retained earnings: A document that reflects the amount of income received for the fiscal year.

Statement of revenue and expenditures: A document showing the amount of profit earned minus the amount of operating expenses. The difference is reported as a profit or loss.

Statement of stockholder's equity: An indication of how the stockholder's shares in the company performed over the financial year. Income and losses are reported as well as investment transactions.

States of nature: When a company struggles with fiscal responsibilities. There is a chance this situation will repeat again for the next year.

Static (fixed) budget: A recognition that a current operating mechanism will go through without any changes.

Statistic: The measurement of a unit in the production process.

Statutory audit: This method applies to local town governments that must provide an account of their business practices and policies.

Step allocation method: The process of assigning costs to several different areas in the operations of a business or corporation.

Step costs: An amount assigned to each level in the manufacturing process.

Step-down method: The process of balancing a budget by reducing the number of expenses in several ways. At the high point, the goal is to reduce expenditures on demanded items. At the lowest point, the goal is to reduce expenditures on the least-desired items.

Stock certificate: This paper shows how much a stockholder has invested in a company.

Stock company: An organization that holds shares with exclusive properties.

Stock dividend: When a stockholder receives a portion of his or her claim in a company. Depending on the company, the dividends can be distributed each quarter of the year, twice per year, or once a year.

Stock index futures: The amount of share issues to be traded on the stock market.

Stock option: See *Option.*

Stock outstanding: The amount of stock in possession of shareholders.

Stock register: The information pertaining to shares of stock issued by a company.

Stock right: See *Option.*

Stock split: If a stock is performing well, the stock will be divided to boost the amount of shares.

Stock-out costs: The amount of a loss the company will expense because of a reduction in revenue due to the number of unsold goods.

Stock: A share in the company's equity.

Stockholder of record: A company that is authorized to sell shares of the company's stock.

Stockholder: An individual who has ownership of assets of a company.

Stockholder's equity: This amount represents what the stockholder owns after liabilities are cleared from the company's accounts.

Stockholder's report: See *Statement of stockholder's equity.*

Stop-loss order: The option to purchase or issue a stock when it falls below a comparable market price.

Stop-payment order: A financial institution will initiate the ability to not authorize funds to be paid for a product or service.

Stores: The amount of a company's inventory that does not affect direct or indirect costs.

Straight-line depreciation: This type of action is the widely accepted method in accounting. To utilize this method, you need to determine the asset price divided by the life of the asset.

Straight-line method: Noted as the most widely recognized way to depreciate tangible goods.

Stranded asset: A valued instrument that is not performing well in the stock market but must be kept on a financial statement in order to record a loss of profit.

Strike price: An investor will set a specified amount to sell his or her stock.

Subordinated debt: A loan that does not carry a high value to retain assets and earnings.

Subsidiary account: An account used to describe the business activity that is associated with a particular balance sheet account.

Subsidiary ledger: The area where the company allocates client transactions to match with the company details of purchases or sales.

Subscribed stock: Investments that were purchased on an incremental payment plan.

Substance over form: Auditors try to use this accounting method to determine costs based on which assets and liabilities are used instead of how these assets and liabilities are categorized. Although this is a legal practice, this method is scrutinized because companies can hide the background information on certain assets and liabilities that are questionable under GAAP standards.

Sum-of-the-year's digits method: This determines a faster rate of depreciation by how many years the asset as been in use.

Sunk cost: Also referred to as a *Historical cost.*

Supernormal growth: When a stock or bond reaches a high point of return due to situations affecting the country's economic status. For example, if an engineering firm experiences a stock boom during a growth in the construction industry.

Suspense account: A temporary place for transactions until a company figures out where the cost needs to be transferred.

Supplies: Items used in business operations, such as office pens and paper.

Supplies expense: The account that is used when supplies are bought for business operations.

Supplies on hand: This term is also referred to as supplies.

Support costs: Also referred to as *Operating cost.*

Surcharge: Another charge added to a bill or purchase order. For example, freight charges for the shipment of goods to a foreign country.

Surplus: See *Economic surplus.*

Surrender value: This applies to a life insurance policy that becomes due or has been terminated and must be paid in cash.

Suspense account: A temporary place for transactions until a company figures out where the cost needs to be transferred.

Switching costs: The amount of money a customer will lose when he or she decides to change from one department store to another.

Synthetic asset: The combination of one investment and other investment. For example, putting together a stock that has a "call" option and a stock that has a "put" option.

CHAPTER 22

DEFINITIONS

T-account: The traditional way to record a debit and credit in one account shaped like a "T." The long line is for the account name, the left column is the debit amount, and the right column is the credit amount.

Take-home pay: The amount an employee receives minus required deductions. The deductions include taxes, health care benefits, and employee contributions to pensions or retirement funds.

Take or pay agreement: A contract between two individual parties that requires payment for services, although the services are not rendered at a certain time. An example of a take or pay agreement is a contract with an electric company.

Takeover: A company will try to gain full ownership rights of another company.

Tangible assets: A valued instrument in a company's business operations, like money and equipment.

Tangible book value: The current value of an investment on the trading market will be given to an investor if a company is no longer conducting business operations.

Tangible constructed asset: A valued instrument that has associated depreciable costs. One example of a tangible constructed asset is a piece of equipment in the warehouse.

Tangible cost: The amount assigned to an area of business operations, such as payment for supplies.

Target cash balance: How much money a company needs to have to maintain business operations.

Target income: The amount of revenue a company wants to generate for the current accounting period.

Target interest rate: Also referred to as a *Hurdle rate*.

Target leverage ratio: The amount of money a company can safely pay off for expenses without compromising the amount of revenue earned.

Target payout ratio: The amount of money a company wants to have to be able to pay dividends to investors.

Target price: (1) The amount for which an investor wants to sell his or her shares of stock, or (2) how much a vendor calculates that a consumer will buy a particular product.

Tariff: Replaced by the Federal Income Tax accounting system, this type of tax was imposed on any imports or exports within the United States. Currently, this tax is still used in many other countries.

Tax-effect accounting: The appropriation of income taxes during the time the taxes incurred, instead of when the taxes need to be paid.

Tax-equivalent yield: The amount of taxes calculated on an investment that matches the taxes incurred on an investment made through a municipality.

Tax accounting: The management of accounting practices that incorporate tax laws. This type of accounting is regulated by the IRS.

Tax base: The amount of taxes that will be charged based on the value of the assets of an individual or corporation.

Tax credit: An allowance to be subtracted from adjusted income. Childcare expenses are an example of a tax credit.

Tax deed: If tax payments have not been made on a property, an agreement is issued for another individual to take ownership of the property.

Tax depreciation: Also referred to as the *Modified ACRS*.

Tax evasion: When an individual or a corporation deliberately does not report the correct amount of taxes incurred on reported income to the Internal Revenue Service.

Tax lien: When an individual fails to make a payment on a property, there will be judgment placed against the individual to repay the amount, including outstanding interest and taxes.

Tax loss carry back/forward: The ability to reduce the amount of a tax burden on an individual or corporation if there is a reported loss in the current accounting period. The IRS allows an individual or corporation the ability to carry back for the prior 3 years.

Tax rate schedule: A document for taxpayers that shows how much in taxes should be paid based on their filing status, for example if they are single or married.

Tax reform: The way the government revises how tax laws are imposed.

Tax return: The form that an individual or corporation utilizes to show how much in taxes will be paid according to income earned.

Tax shelter: A legal form of trying to reduce the tax burden based on how much income has been earned. An example of a tax shelter is an employee contribution like a 401(k).

Tax shield: The ability of an individual or corporation to reduce the amount of taxes to be paid by taking certain tax breaks. These breaks include donations to charities, medical, or childcare expenses.

Tax year: The timeframe used to file a tax return. This timeframe varies based on the filing status of an individual, business, or corporation.

Tax: To charge an individual or corporation an amount to support local and federal business operations.

Taxable benefits: Non-monetary compensation that is received by an employee. One example of a taxable benefit is health insurance.

Taxable income: The amount the federal government requires to be reported yearly on a tax return. The amount is computed by taking expenses and allowed deductions from the total amount of income earned.

Taxes payable: When taxes need to be paid out by the company, the company will record the amount of taxes in a payable account, such as the income taxable payable account.

Telephone expense: The account that records payments for communication services, like fax machine service.

Temporary account: A method used for income and expenses for a particular time. Once the company's financial year ends, these accounts are converted to an equity account.

Temporary help expense: When a company employs contract workers for a short period of time, the company records the amount paid to the individuals in this type of account.

Temporary investments: This transaction is done when a business owner makes a loan to another individual. The lender accounts for this transaction as a credit on the balance statement.

Tender offer: When a company is in the process of acquiring another company, the company will request that the other company accepts an agreement to give shares to a comparable market price.

Tenor of a draft: Payment that is made at the time a document is signed.

Term bond: When a bond reaches maturity.

Terminal value: How much an investment is worth when the investment reaches its maturity date.

Termination benefits: When an employee has been released from his or her duties from a company, the company will give the employee compensation for a specified amount of time. The compensation can include vacation pay, health insurance, and life insurance.

Term endowment: Funds that are given by donation but must be used during a specified time period.

Term insurance: A life insurance policy that expires in a specified amount of time. This is the most common form of life insurance.

Term loans: An agreement made between a financial institution and a third party that outlines when payments will be made on a schedule.

The Accountant's Magazine: A journal that was founded in 1897 by the Aberdeen, Edinburgh, and Glasgow chartered accountants' societies and was adopted by the Institute of Chartered Accountants in Scotland in 1951.

Theory of constraints: Used in cost accounting, this method is based on outlining how to eliminate impacts on production while still increasing the profit margin. Impacts on production can include a decrease in production output because of mechanical difficulties or handling waste products effectively.

Third party: Another individual or group that is not related to the individuals who are engaged in business or activities with other people.

Third party recovery: A group that is hired to recoup monies owed to individuals or businesses.

Tick mark: A notation made by an auditor to show that a review of an accounting sheet has been made.

Time-adjusted rate of return: This is also referred to as *Internal rate of return*.

Time card: This document is prepared to show how many hours an employee worked during a workweek.

Time deposits: Money credited to an account that is not ready for withdrawal until a specified time.

Time draft: Also referred to as a *Sight draft*.

Time interest earned (TIE): This measurement determines how a company can afford to pay operating expenses.

Time period assumption: The amount of money that relates to income and capital gains earned from an investment. The return is adjusted for inflation, and investors can keep it. This is also referred to as the *Time interval concept.*

Time value of money: Involves how money management concepts are utilized in financial accounting practices. A concept can analyze the bond market.

Tombstone: The announcement of a company's desire to issue investments through a brokerage. The information in the announcement is considered a preliminary breakdown of what investments the company will offer.

Total asset turnover: This determines how much of the company's assets are subjected to a change in reporting for the next accounting period.

Total assets: The full amount of the company's assets on the financial statements.

Total cost of ownership: The price of a valued instrument with additional costs to operate the instrument.

Total cost: (1) The addition of all costs — direct and indirect, or (2) how much an investor paid to acquire an investment. The cost includes commissions and trading fees.

Total market value: The amount a stock or bond is worth on the trading market.

Tracking stock: (1) Keeping an eye on stock that was issued by a parent company, or (2) an investment that is created to trade on higher index strategy.

Trade acceptance: An agreement of purchase for a specific item that is signed by both the vendor and consumer.

Trade concern: Individuals or companies expressing the desire to purchase investments on the trading market must make sure the third party is viable before making a purchase.

Trade credit: This is equivalent to an accounts payable account. For example, a firm agrees to pay off a loan at a certain time.

Trade date: The recording of an investment transaction at the time of purchase or sale.

Trade debtors: Investors who still need to pay for their initial investment purchases.

Trade deficit: When the amount of trade expenses outweighs the original trade value.

Trade discount: Goods traded in bulk supply, offered at a reduced price. This rule only applies to individuals authorized to trade.

Trade draft: A document between two companies to initiate a trade.

Trade exchange: The place where investments and securities are listed on the market. The largest trade exchange in the world is the United States Stock Exchange.

Trademark: A way to distinguish the rights to a patent or property of a business or company. For example, the symbol of the letter "R" inside a circle (®) indicates a trademark has been established for a company and could only be used for that company.

Trade name: A business or corporation utilizes this type of identification for purposes of conducting operations on the trading market. This name can be different than the entity's legal name.

Trade payable: This is another name for *Accounts Payable*.

Trade receivables: This is another name for *Accounts Receivable*.

Trading account: An account that is set up by the individual who oversees the investment operations of the company. Investments in stocks or bonds are recorded in this account.

Trading on the equity: Utilizing acquired investments to obtain more investment revenue in order to maximize a higher profit return.

Trading profit: The revenue recognized on a trade that is recorded on the balance sheet for the accounting period in which the trade occurred.

Trailing return: When an investment is compared against another investment for a specific time period to see how much profit has been earned.

Trailing: The evaluation of an investment for a specific time period that cannot go over one year.

Tranches: Derived from the French term tranche, which translates to the word "slice," this term describes a slice of the investment that is not used in the same way as other investments. The slice has a different yield than the rest of the investment.

Transaction: Activities incurred by the act of doing business from one entity to another. These items can range from purchase and sale of goods or services to payments for services rendered.

Transaction risk: When there is a lapse of time between the initial purchase agreement and when the agreement is actually in place, an investor will have a greater chance of dealing with a higher risk due to the daily changes in the market.

Transfer pricing: When costs need to be transferred from one department of a company to another department of a company. For example, the cost for lighting a building is transferred to an administrative department instead of a construction department.

Transferred-in cost: In cost accounting, costs incurred by one department can be moved to another department.

Treasury bill (T-bill): An investment with a maturity that expires one year after the investment has been issued.

Treasury stock: Securities that are repurchased by the corporation who released the first issue of stocks or bonds. Unfortunately, these stocks or bonds carry some downsides — loss of voting power and lower payment of dividends. Many investors choose to stay away from treasury stocks, because they do not have a vote or could yield a low profit.

Trial balance: The method of reporting a company's financial status at any time. The accountant will match the amounts in each of the company's ledger accounts. If the amounts are equal, the calculation is proven successful.

Triple net lease: An agreement where a lessee must pay all costs associated with rental of a building or equipment. The costs include maintenance fees, taxes, and insurance.

True-up: To make sure the totals for each line item matches the appropriate debit or credit account.

True and fair view: Mostly used in the United Kingdom, this term applies to how an auditor will render a decision on the accounting practices of a company.

True value: The price a consumer will pay for a product.

Trust account: An investment set up for an individual that is managed by a third party.

Trust deed: (1) A document that sets forth the terms of a trust account, or (2) to add an additional investment to an existing investment.

Trustee: An individual who is responsible for the ownership of a property for another individual.

Trust receipt: Documentation to support that ownership of a trust is held by the bank but can be used as collateral to purchase new investments.

Turnover ratios: A method to determine how much a company will have to report as unsold and/or unused merchandise or services. An inventory turnover ratio is computed by taking the amount of inventory sold over the amount of inventory left on hand.

Turnover tax: Treated like the *Ad valorem* except for one major difference — this tax is computed on major products and services at the end of the manufacturing process.

CHAPTER 23

DEFINITIONS

Unabsorbed costs: The unused portion of manufacturing costs that cannot be applied to income earned if the production level drops during the manufacturing process.

Unappropriated retained earnings: Like retained earnings, unless part of the profit is held for a special purpose.

Unaudited opinion: A decision made by a Certified Public Accountant who did not prepare a company's financial statements but was called in to give an unbiased statement about the company's financial status.

Uncollected funds: When a business or company does not receive payment because the customer did not have enough money in his or her bank account to pay for the goods or services.

Uncollectible accounts expense: When a business or company does not receive payment for goods or services, the transaction must be recorded as an expense for unpaid balance.

Underwriter: An individual who is responsible for maintaining investments for a third party.

Unearned premium revenue: The account that holds the amount of income to be recognized for insurance premiums until the policies have become due.

Unearned revenue: The business or corporation will record a profit for goods and services that have not been sold or provided to another individual or business.

Unemployment compensation tax: This is similar to the *Federal Unemployment Tax Act (FUTA)* except this tax is state regulated. This tax represents the amount an employer deducts from an employee's salary to compensate for benefits if an employee becomes unemployed.

Unfavorable variance: The difference between the amount of production and projected costs. If actual production costs are higher than the projected costs, the company has an undesirable rate for production.

Unit value: The amount a business or corporation is worth. This term applies to businesses or corporations that deal with public or private utilities, such as a municipal water department.

Units of production method of depreciation: Instead of a traditional method of depreciation, this method utilizes the amount of units that are available for sale compared to how much time it took for the units to be produced. This is also referred to as the *Units of activity method of deprecation*.

Unleveraged: When a company will use funds within the company to purchase investments instead of borrowing from another source.

Unlimited liability: A business or corporation gives up rights to assets under this type of organization. When a company needs to sell off assets, shareholders can claim their stake first.

Unlisted stock: Investments that are traded on the OTC (over-the-counter) exchange.

Unpaid principal balance: The amount of money that must be paid on the principal amount of the loan.

Unqualified audit: An assessment of a company that is considered to be accurate.

Unqualified opinion: A statement made by an auditor that is considered to be true after review of a company's financial statements.

Unrealized holding gain/loss: An income or expense that must be reported after a company relinquishes property that has been active in business operations.

Unrecorded expenses: When a company sells a product but has not received income. The company records this transaction until the payment is made.

Unrecorded revenue: The amount is allocated as income but no payment has been made. In order to consider these transactions as a profit, an accountant must perform a line item adjustment to the balance sheet.

Unsecured bond: Also referred to as a *Debenture bond*.

Unsecured creditor: A lender who will receive payment for goods or services not based on a hold against personal property.

Unusual but not extraordinary item: An asset or liability that must be included on financial statements but that does not meet the necessary reporting requirements. This happens when a company suffers a loss due to a labor dispute. The company must report the loss on a different part of the financial statement, not where normal income and expenses are reported.

Usage variance: Also referred to as *Direct materials usage variance.*

Useful life: The length of time equipment will be operable for business operations.

Utilities expense: The cost of usage of utilities such as lighting, water, and heat. These expenses are included on all financial statements.

Utilities payable: When a business or company has to pay for the cost of utilities, an accountant will record how much is paid in this account.

CHAPTER 24

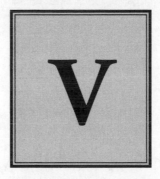

DEFINITIONS

Vacation pay expense: The amount of money paid to an employee for vacation time.

Vacation pay payable: How much will be paid to an employee for vacation time to occur at a future date.

Valuation account: This is an account with dual purposes to be used for expenses related to receivables and depreciation.

Valuation reserve: An account used to offset a decline in profit earnings during times of economic stress. For example, an allowance for bad debts.

Valuation: The method of equating an asset to a liability on a company's ledger.

Value billing: The amount that is charged for services based on the price of the service instead of how much time was dedicated to the project.

Variable committed expense: An unavoidable expense that changes throughout the business year. This type of expense can be a heating and air conditioning cost or building maintenance cost.

Variable costs: The expenses of operating a business that change in direct proportion to the business' activity.

Variable cost ratio: The assessment of the amount of manufacturing costs related to how much sales revenue has been recognized.

Variable costing: This method differs from calculating a cost related to the absorption method. To utilize this method, an accountant factors in associated costs involved in the manufacturing process.

Variable expenses: Costs of manufacturing that can change throughout the business year. Examples of such expenses are electric costs and sales commissions.

Variable manufacturing overhead applied: Instead of using direct labor and manufacturing costs, variable costs are utilized to determine how much overhead will be used during the manufacturing process.

Variable manufacturing efficiency variance: Instead of using direct labor costs, variable costs are utilized to determine the quality of the products that were produced during the manufacturing process.

Variable manufacturing overhead incurred: Like the term *Variable manufacturing overhead applied*, direct labor costs are utilized to determine how much overhead was actually used during the manufacturing process.

Variance: The comparison of how much it will cost to manufacture a product over how much the company projected it would cost to manufacture a product.

Vertical analysis: An assessment of financial statements in which you take the total number of sales and convert the number to a percentage of goods sold.

Vertical merger: A company tries to acquire another company with a similar business structure. For example, an ice cream manufacturer aligning with a company that processes ice cream toppings.

Vested interest: When an employee makes a payment into a pension plan, the payment is allocated toward the interest in the plan.

Vetting: When an investor is checking out a potential investment before he or she decides to make a purchase or bid.

Volume discount: A reduction in the cost of an item if a customer purchases more of that particular item in one sales transaction.

Volume variance: Also referred to as *Fixed manufacturing overhead budget variance.*

Volume: In cost accounting, this term refers to the number of hours it takes to manufacture a product or how much it will cost to produce one unit in one hour.

Voting right: The ability of a stockholder to make decisions based on how much the stockholder has invested in the company.

Voucher system: The method of recording how much money is being used to pay for transactions; it can be cash or check.

Voucher: The record and receipt of payment for a transaction.

CHAPTER 25

DEFINITIONS

Wage and tax statement: Most commonly referred to as a W-2. This form shows the amount of an individual's earnings and deductions.

Wages expense: This account is used when a company pays an employee for his or her work during that accounting period.

Wages payable: This account is used to record employee compensation that has not yet been received by the employee.

Wages: Used in cost accounting, this term refers to how much an employee in a manufacturing business receives for work or services performed.

Warranty expense: When a sale transaction has occurred with a warranty purchase, the vendor will record this expense in the event the product needs to be repaired.

Warranty payable: This is a projection of how much it will cost to fix a product if a consumer purchased a warranty for the product. This term is also referred to as a *warranty liability*.

Warranty: When a consumer purchases a product, he or she may elect to pay for a plan to fix or replace that product if the product becomes damaged or unusable.

Wash sale: Unloading investments that are not performing well and then repurchasing the same investments at a future date. The benefit of this transaction is to help achieve a lower tax deduction on the loss incurred by the bad investment. This is considered a legal transaction.

Wash trade: This is not the same as the methodology behind a wash sale. This practice is not legal, because it deals with selling off and repurchasing investments just to create an increase on the trading market and costs to purchase stocks.

Wear and tear: The normal aging process on equipment or supplies that are used during manufacturing.

Weighted average method: This amount represents how many products or services were created in relation to the amount of sales recorded on the company's general ledger.

Whole life insurance: An insurance policy that carries a cash payoff scale. This policy differs from a term policy, because a term policy does not give cash payments.

With approved credit (WAC): A financial transaction will be recorded once it has been made known that the consumer has the funds to pay for the transaction.

Withholdings: Amounts taken from an individual's income to decrease the amount of taxes owed. One example of a withholding is a federal tax exemption.

Worker compensation insurance: A policy to protect an employee who has been injured on the job.

Worker compensation insurance expense: The amount a company allocates to cover costs associated with claims related to an employee's injury.

Worker compensation insurance payable: The account that holds the amounts paid for an employee's work-related injury.

Working capital: In the short term, this reflects the amount of revenue minus expenses for a company to run efficiently.

Working capital ratio: To figure out how much working capital a company needs to stay in business, the ratio is computed by taking the value of assets minus the value of liabilities.

Work-in-process inventory (WIP): The segment in the manufacturing process that has not been finished or recorded as a processed product or service.

Worksheet: The record of a company's transactions.

Wrap account: An investment account set up by a brokerage firm. The firm charges a set fee to manage the account. The biggest advantage to this type of account is that investors will be burdened with excess fees for trading or administration.

Write-down: The amount that is taken from the actual value of an asset.

Write-off: To reduce an account down to zero in order to close a current accounting period. An example of a write-off is an accounts receivable account.

Write-up/write-up work: An accountant will process a company's financial statements without going through a formal audit review.

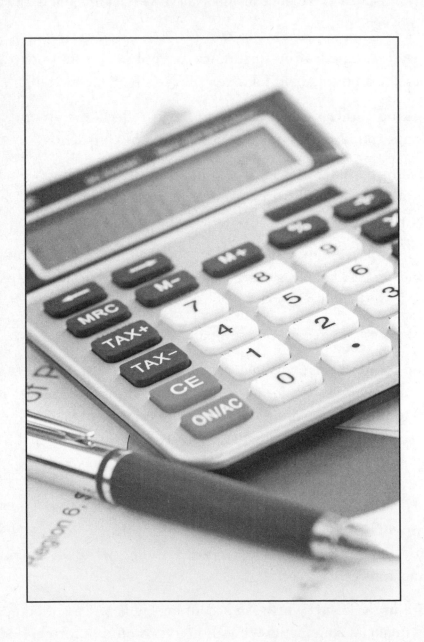

CHAPTER 26

DEFINITIONS

Year over year (YOY): The evaluation of a company's performance based on reviewing the prior year's financial statement with the current year financial statement.

Year to date (YTD): Based on the beginning of the calendar year to a specified date.

Year to date net income: Revenue recognized for a company from the beginning of the calendar year to a specified date.

Yellow knight: A company that was interested in taking over another company but now wants to form a merger with the company.

Yield: The amount of income recognized on an investment.

Yield on cost (YOC): This represents the amount of dividends that will yield above the cost of the total investment.

Yield to call (YTC): The amount that an investment is worth if the investment was not bought or sold until the call option was exercised.

Yield to maturity (YTM): The amount of income recognized on an investment when the investment has reached the end date.

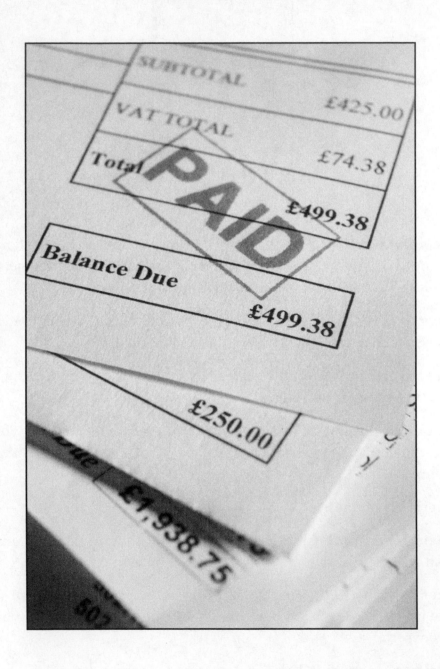

CHAPTER 27

DEFINITIONS

Z: This letter represents a symbol that is used on the NASDAQ trading market. The symbol is used to highlight whether the transaction has a receipt tied to it, or how many units of the stock are available for purchase.

Z-bond: An investment that gains no interest on the coupon when the bond matures.

Zero balance account: This account is maintained when a company handles endorsements with a large amount.

Zero-basis risk swap (ZEBRA): When a municipal stock is traded for another financial security.

Zero coupon bond: A security with a set pay amount that will be redeemed when the bond reaches maturity.

Zero growth stock: When a stock has a return of a definite amount until the stock reaches maturity.

Zero-proof bookkeeping: Used in smaller businesses or for individual purposes, this method of keeping an eye on the books allows for the accounts to have a balance of zero at the end of the accounting period.

Zero uptick: A transaction made at the same price as the one directly preceding it, but at a higher price than the one before that.

Zombies: Businesses that are struggling to maintain daily operations but do not have a positive cash flow to pay liabilities.

BIBLIOGRAPHY

Principles of Accounting: 5th Edition, Anderson, Caldwell and Needles, 1993.

Accounting Coach: **www.accountingcoach.com**

Investopedia: **www.investopedia.com**

Investor Words: **www.investorwords.com**

INDEX